Learn How To Draw Your Favorite Star Wars Characters

Ultimate Guide to Drawing Famous Star Wars Characters

Star Wars

By: Gala Publication

Published By:

Gala Publication

ISBN-13: **978-1522708377**
ISBN-10: **1522708375**

©Copyright 2015 – Gala Publication

INDEX

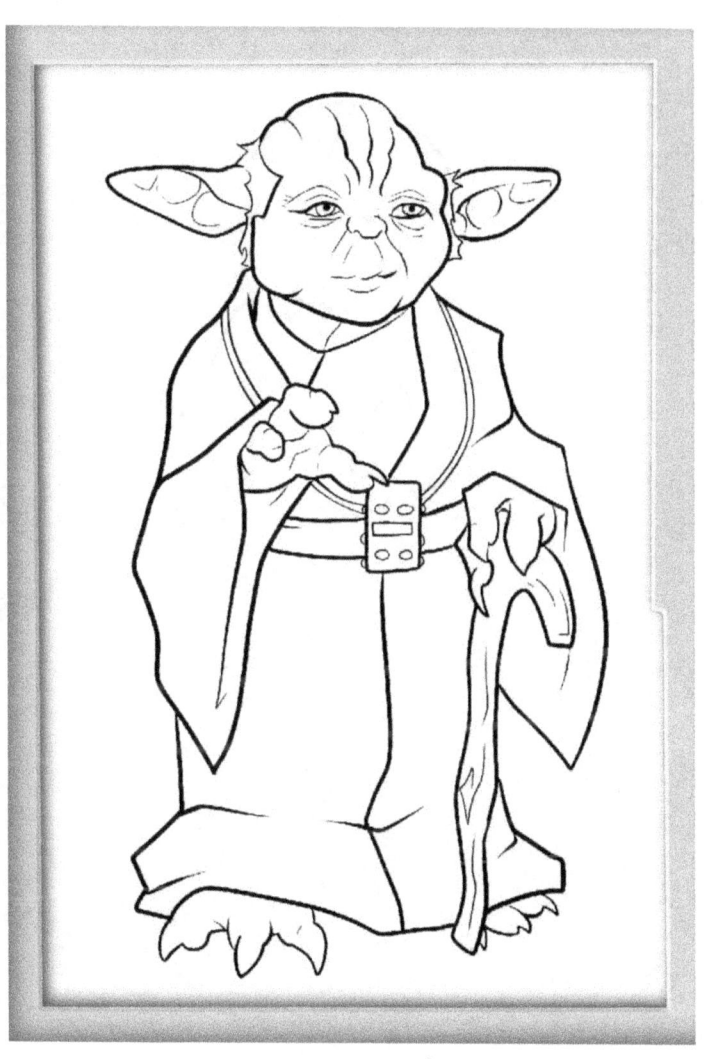

YODA

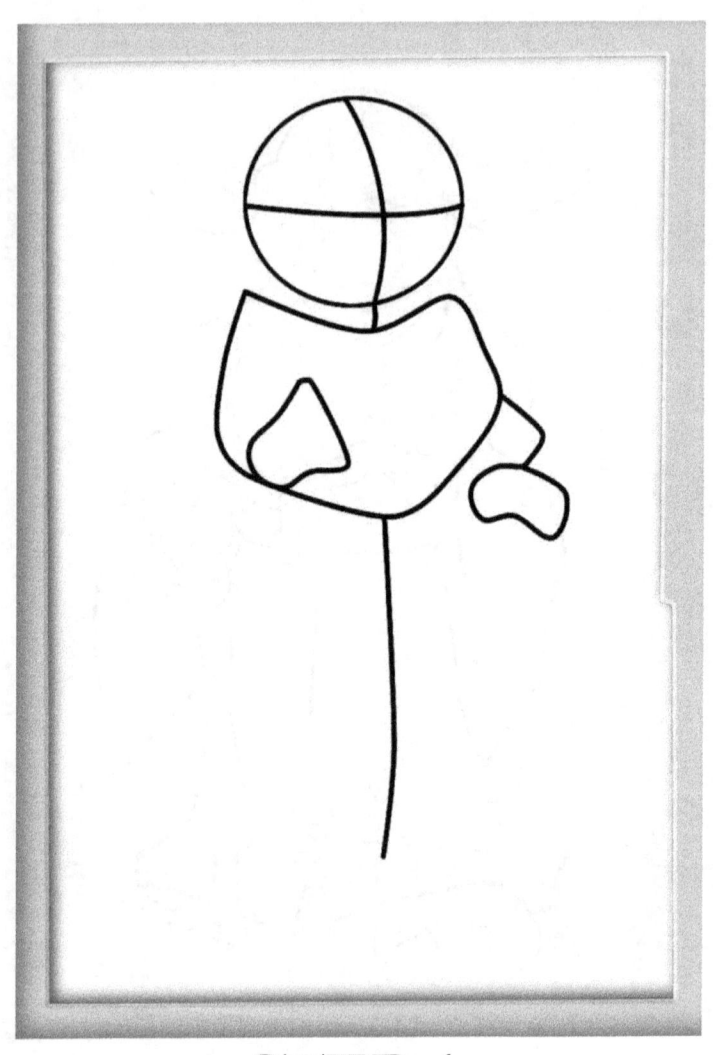

STEP 1

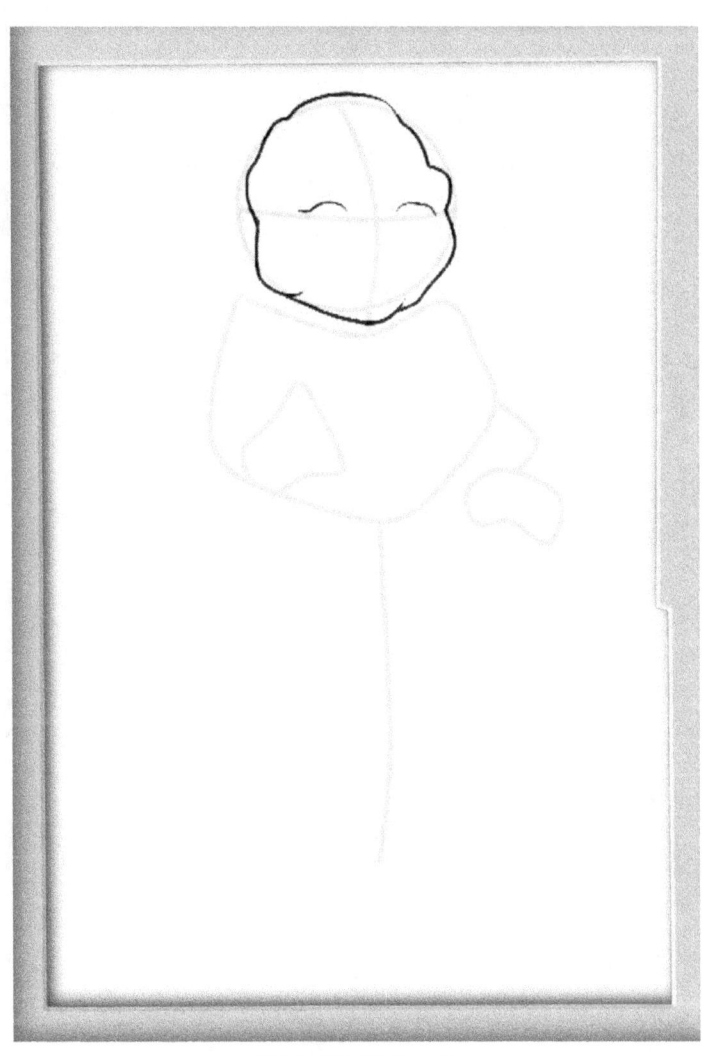

STEP 2

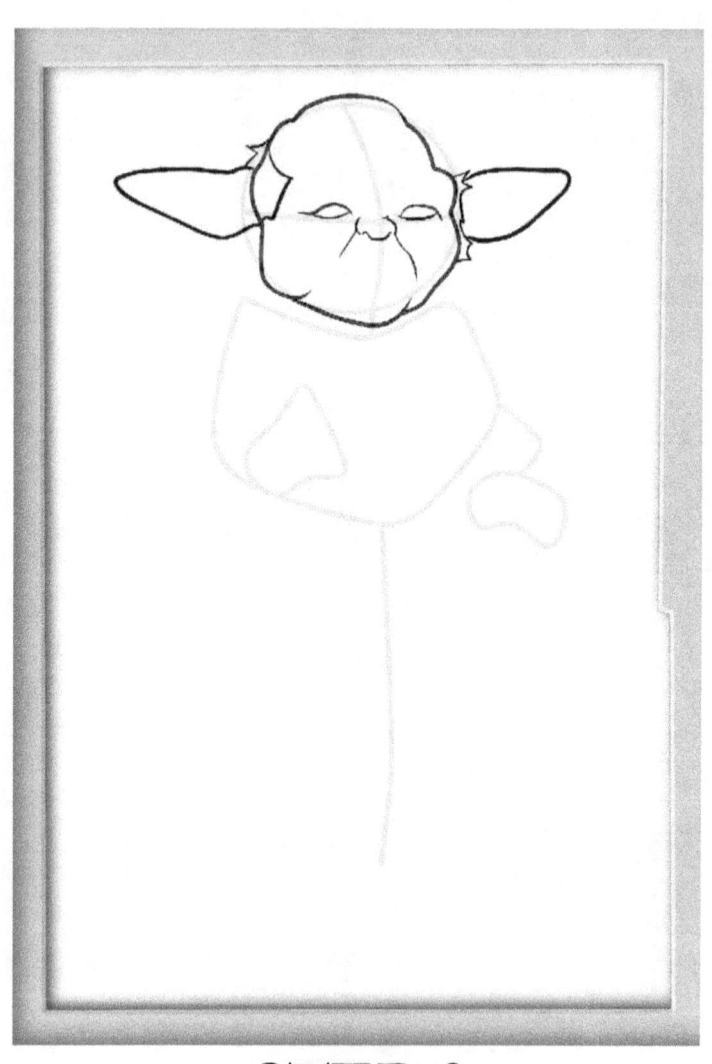

STEP 3

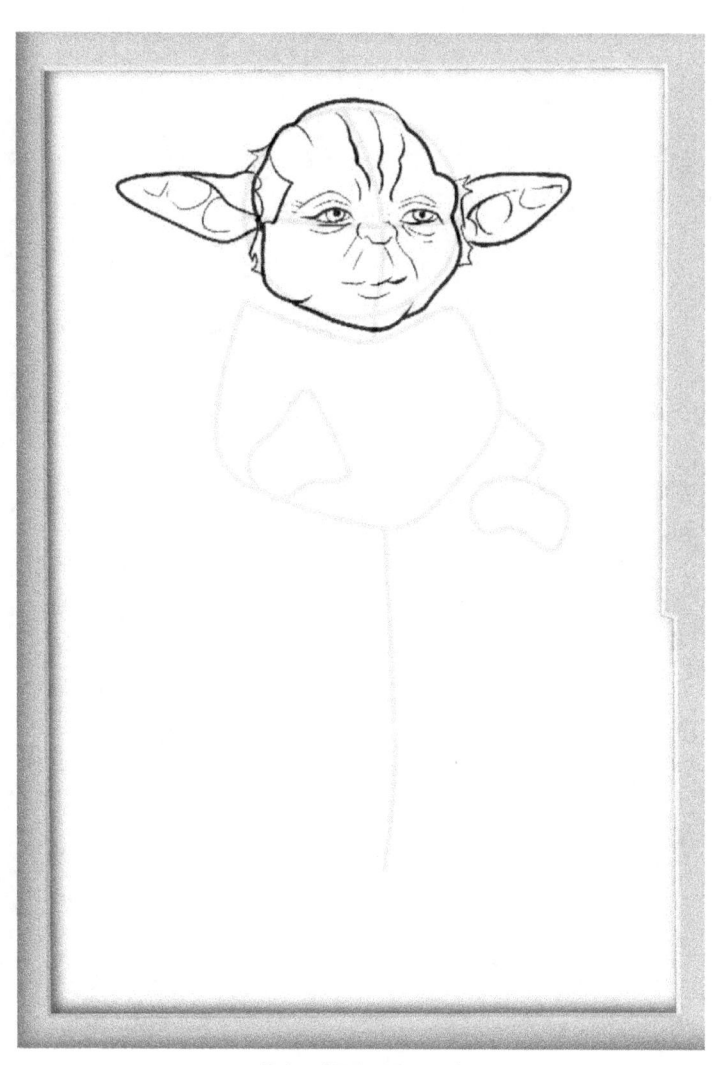

STEP 4

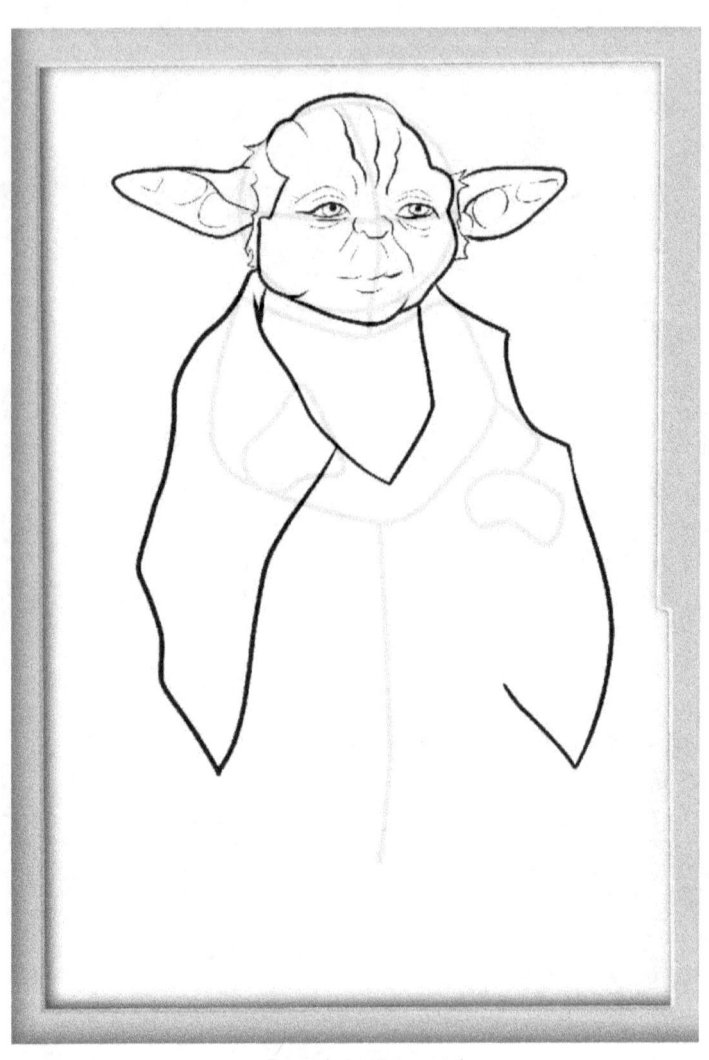

STEP 5

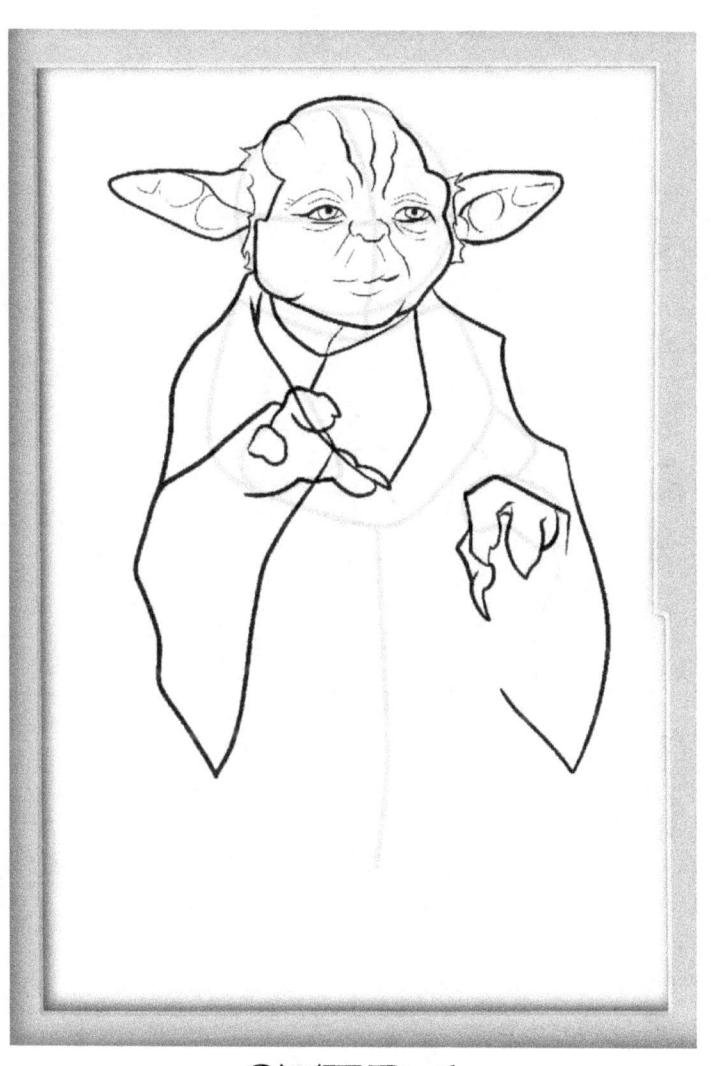

STEP 6

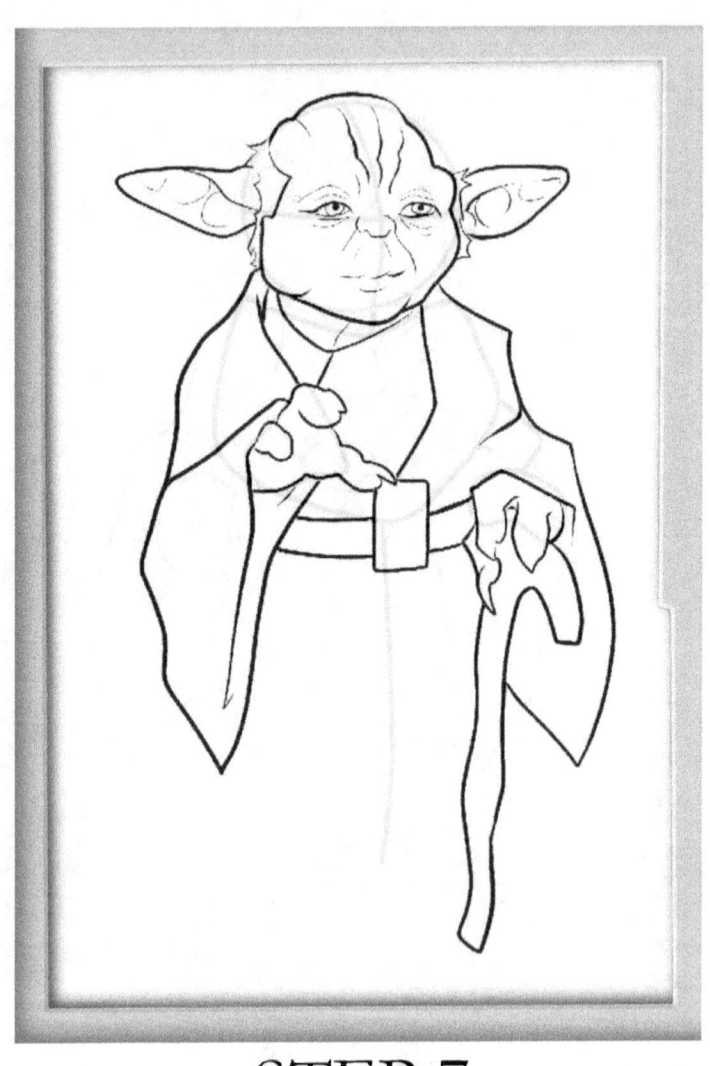

STEP 7

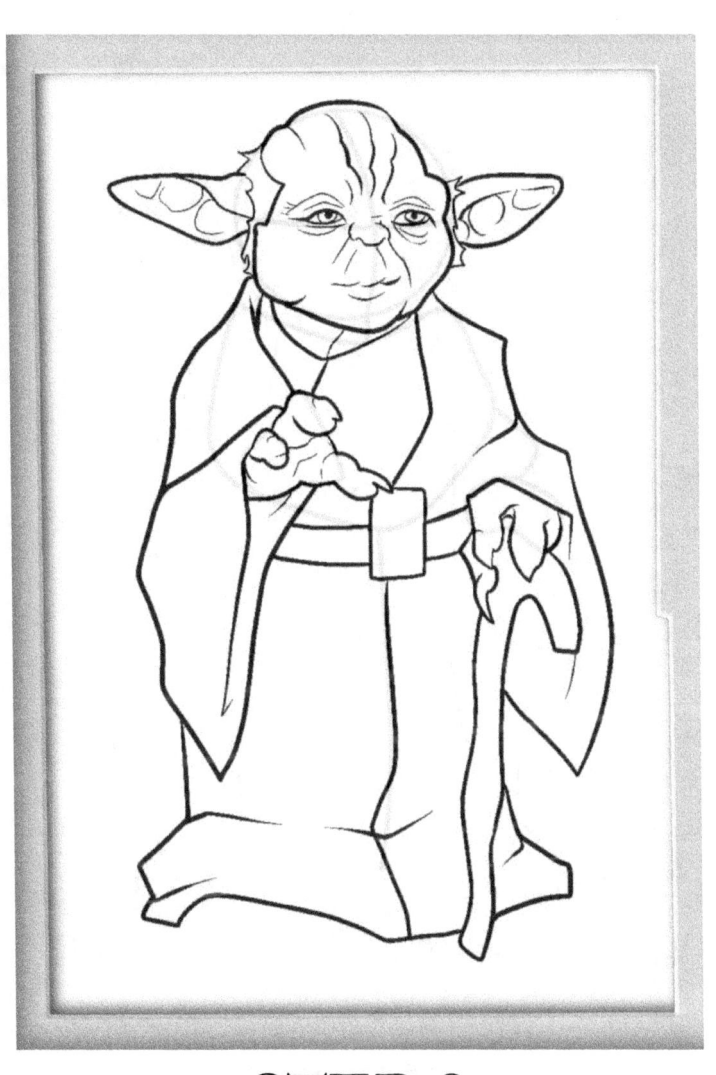

STEP 8

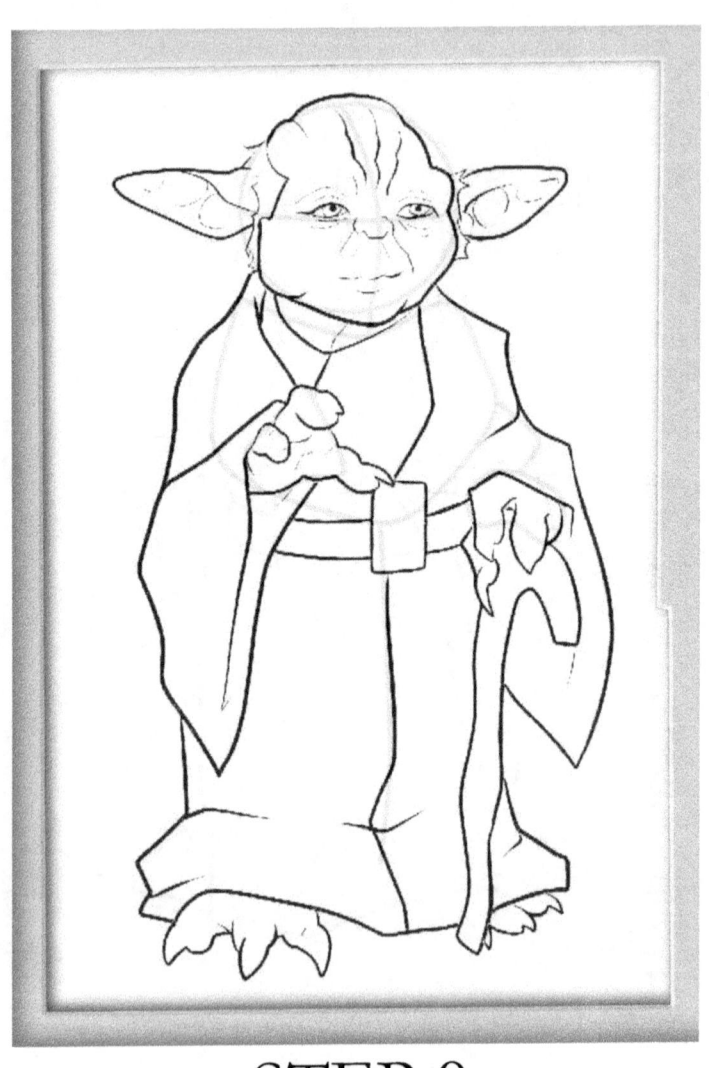

STEP 9

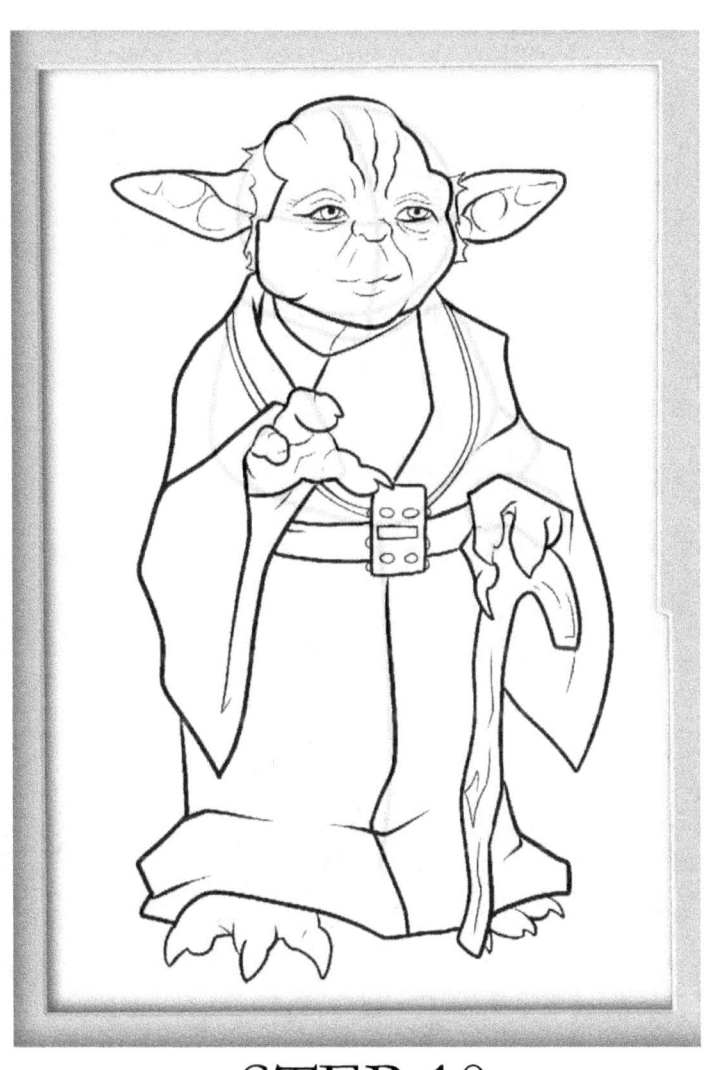

STEP 10

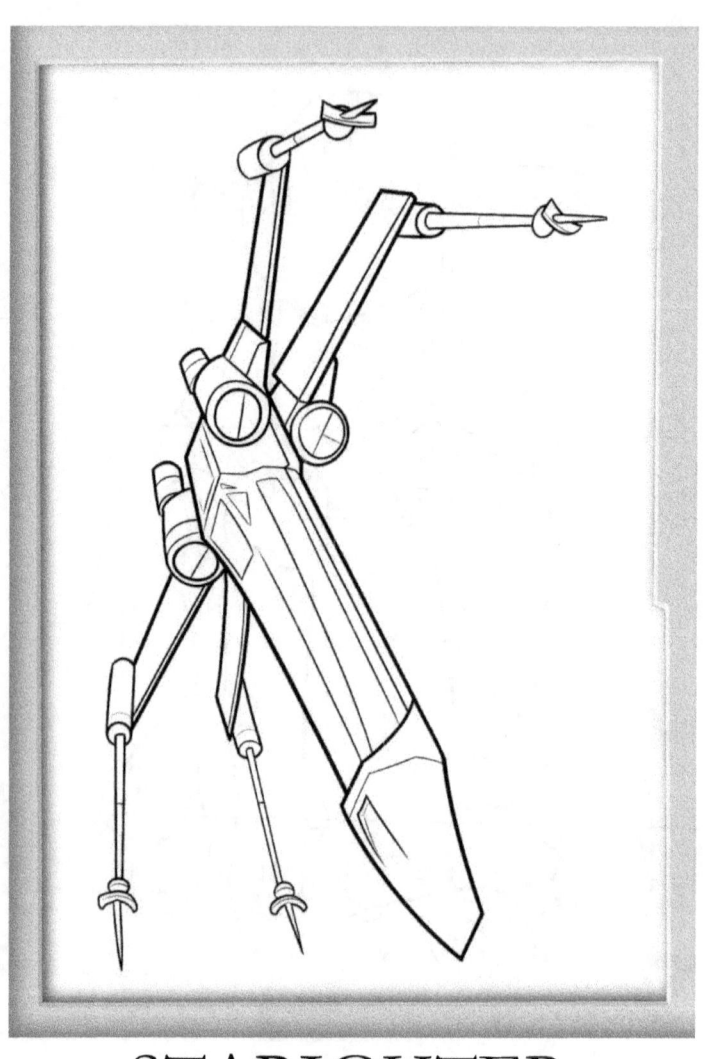

STARIGHTER

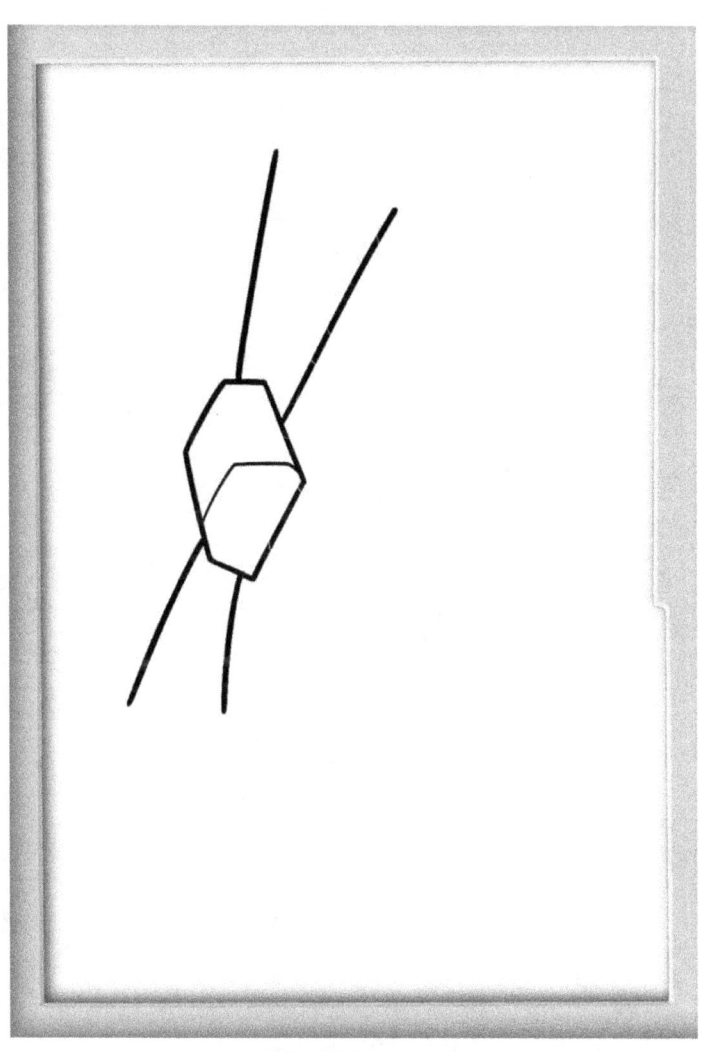

STEP 1

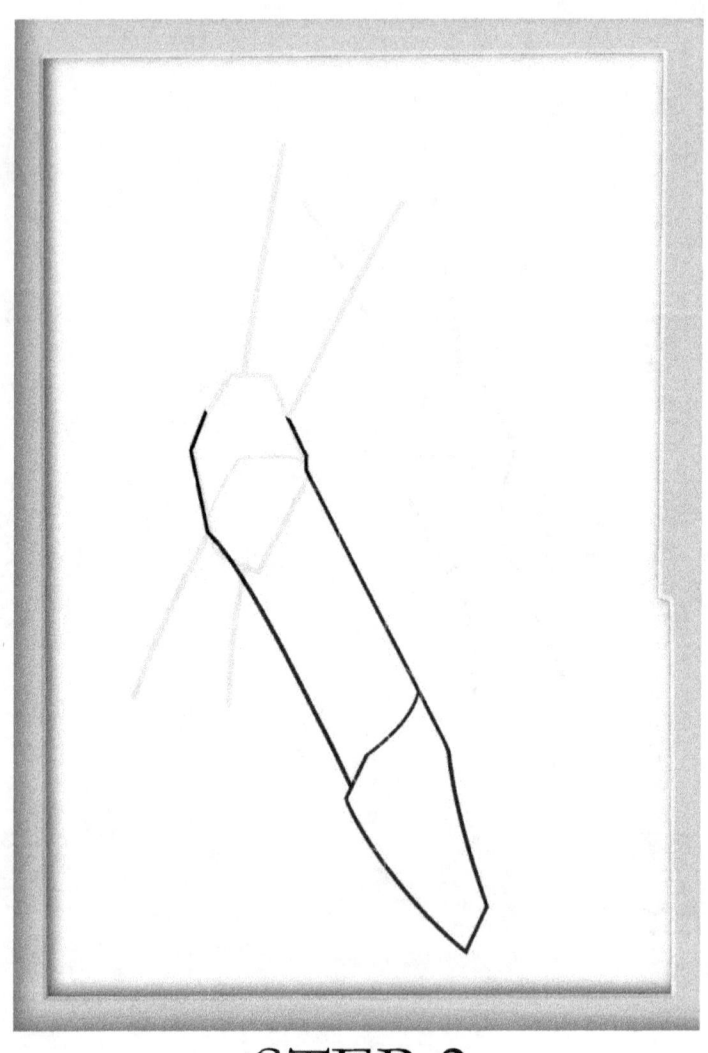

STEP 2

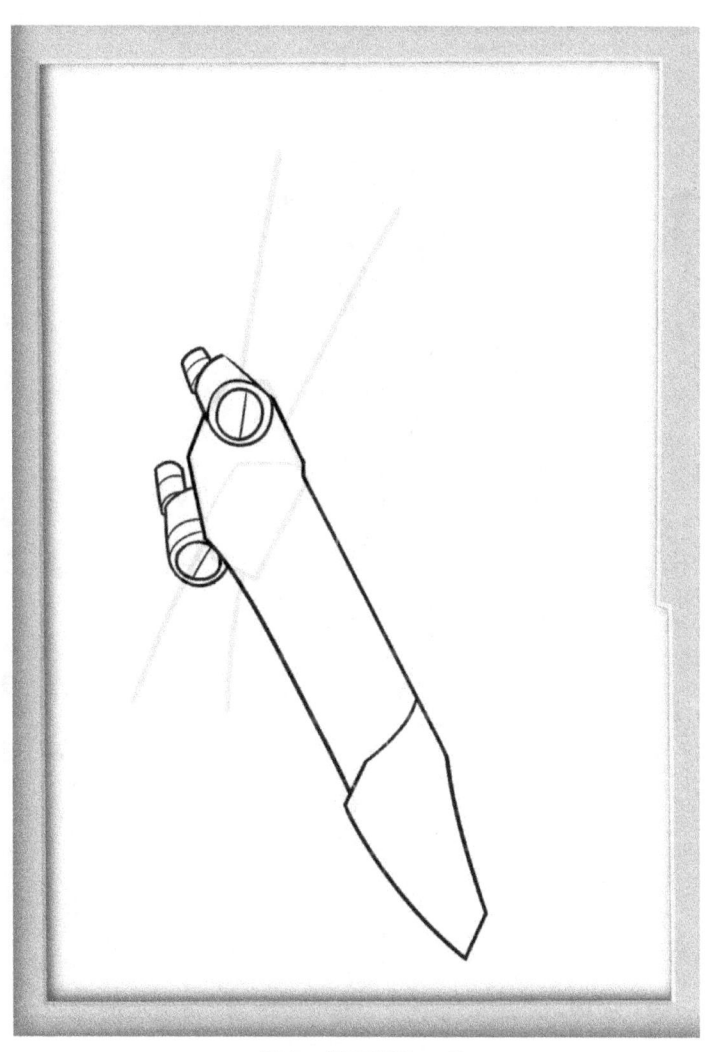

STEP 3

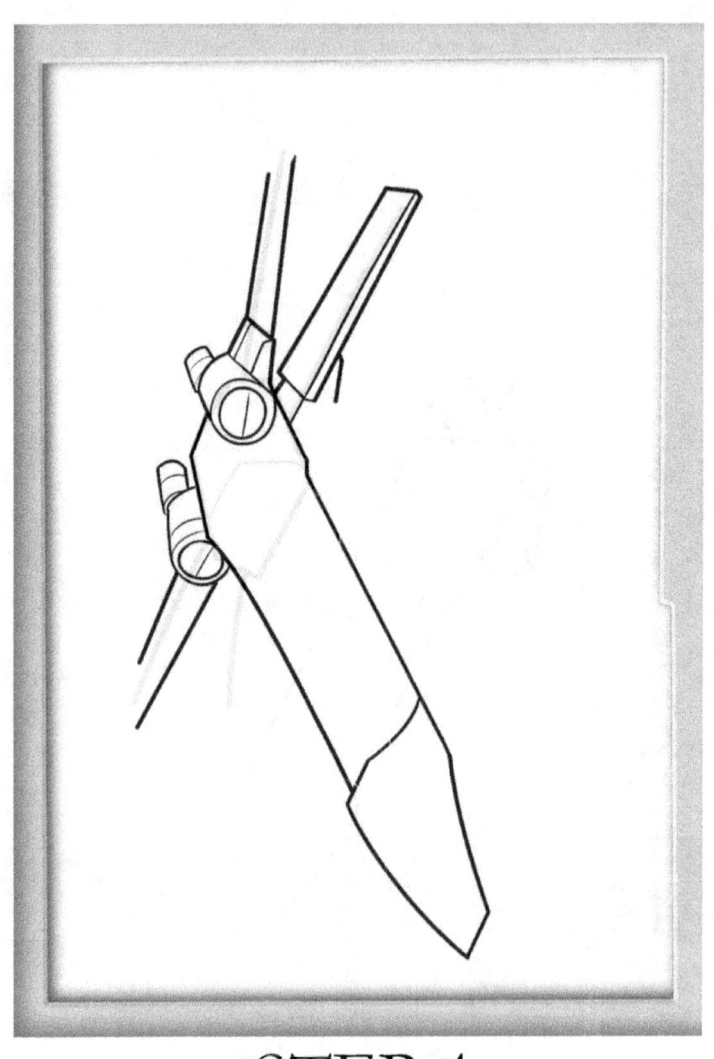

STEP 4

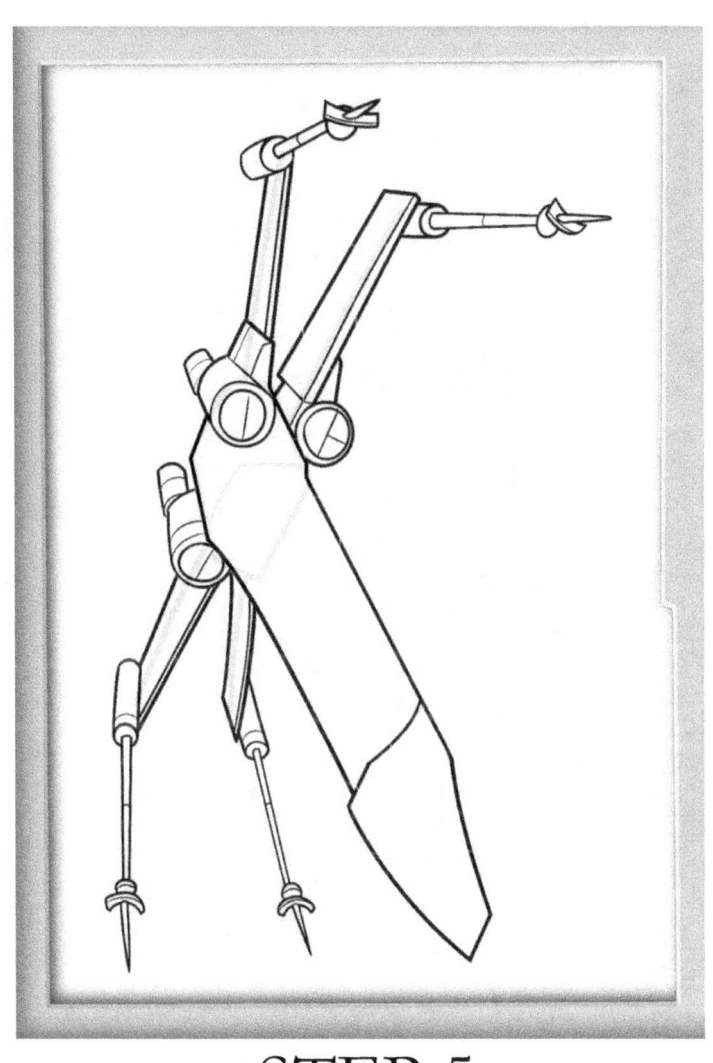

STEP 5

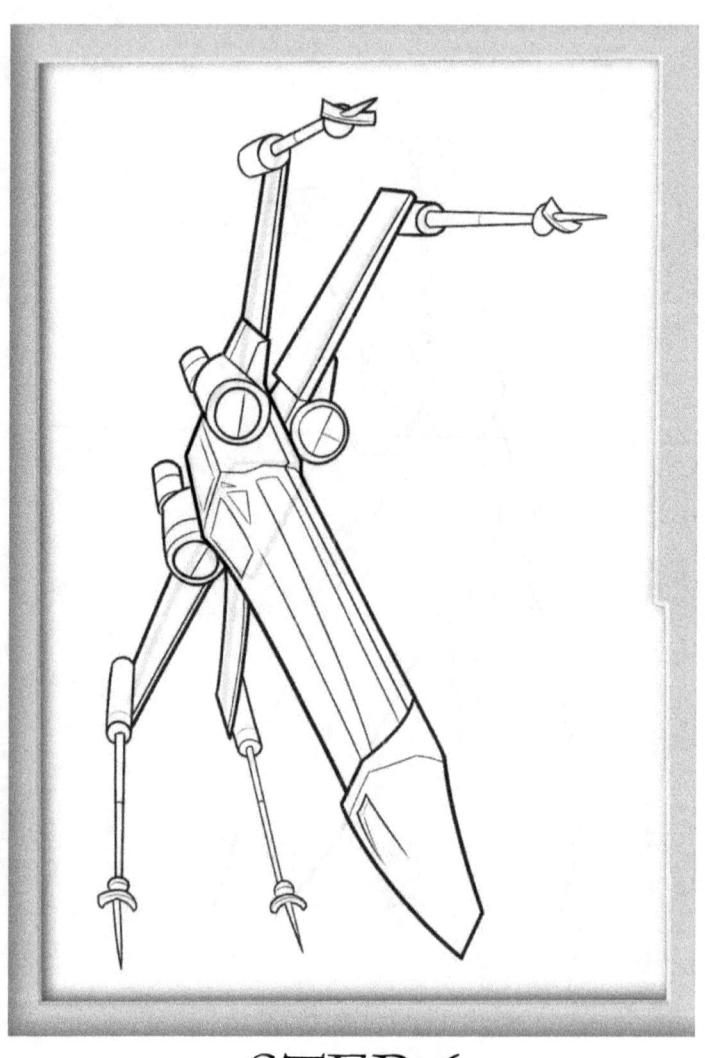

STEP 6

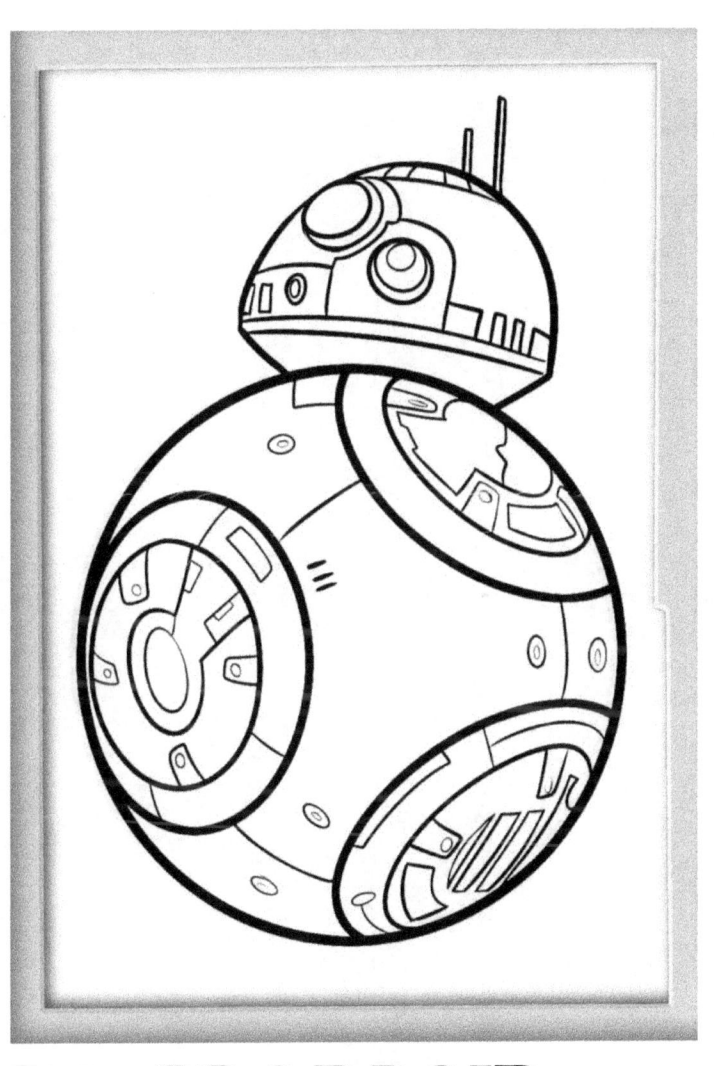

BB 8 DROID

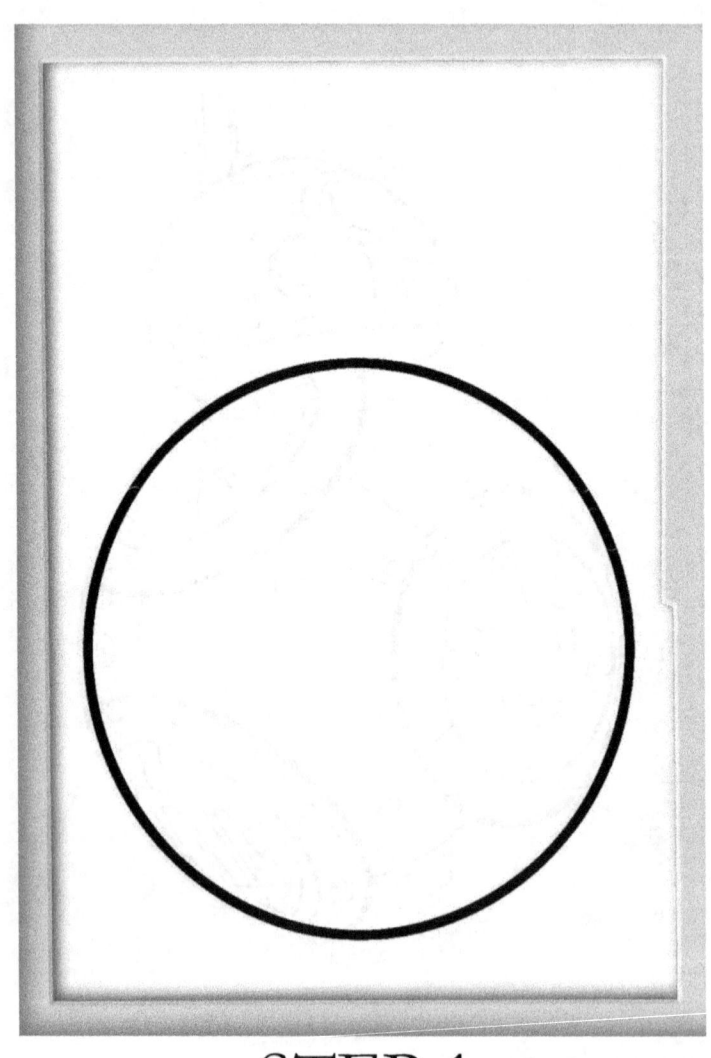

STEP 1

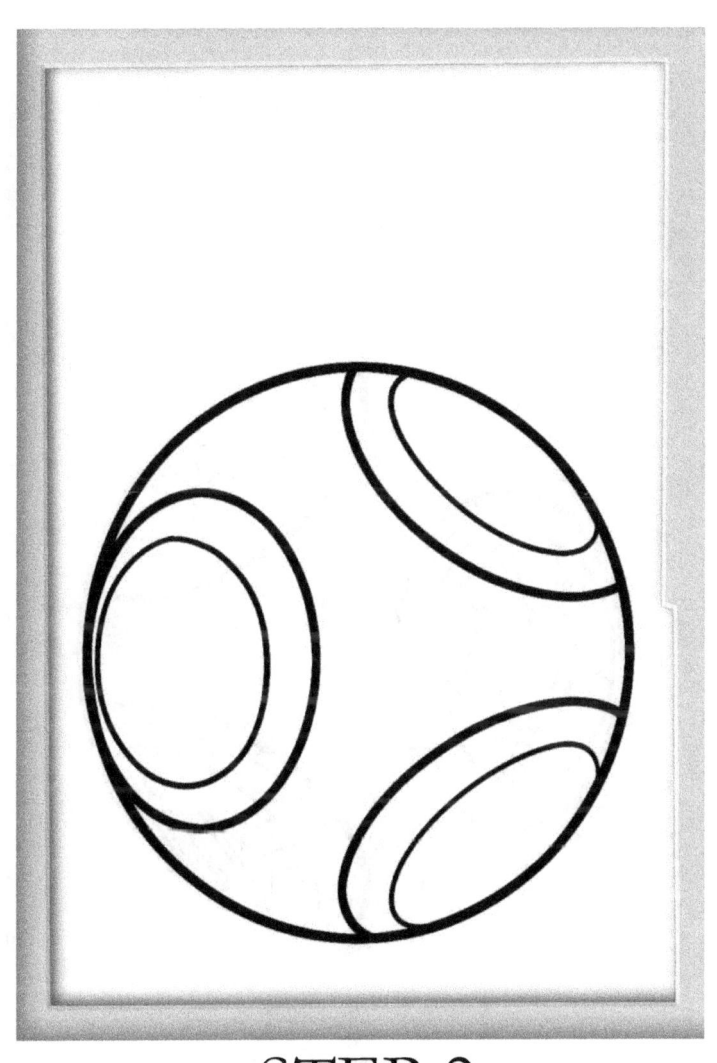

STEP 2

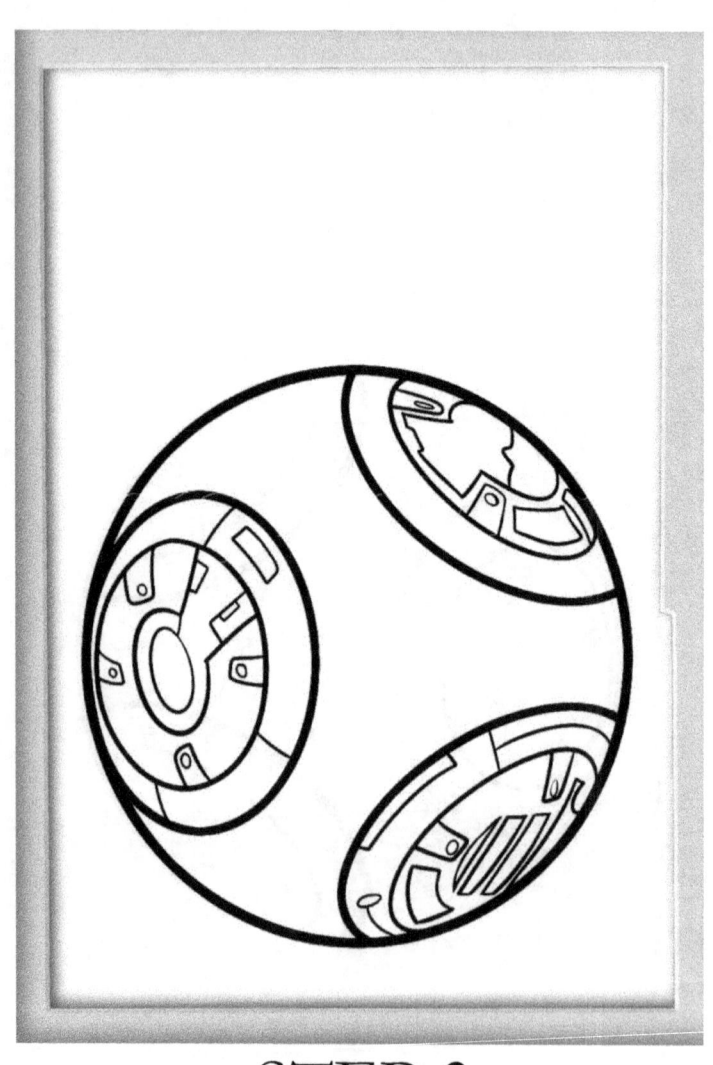

STEP 3

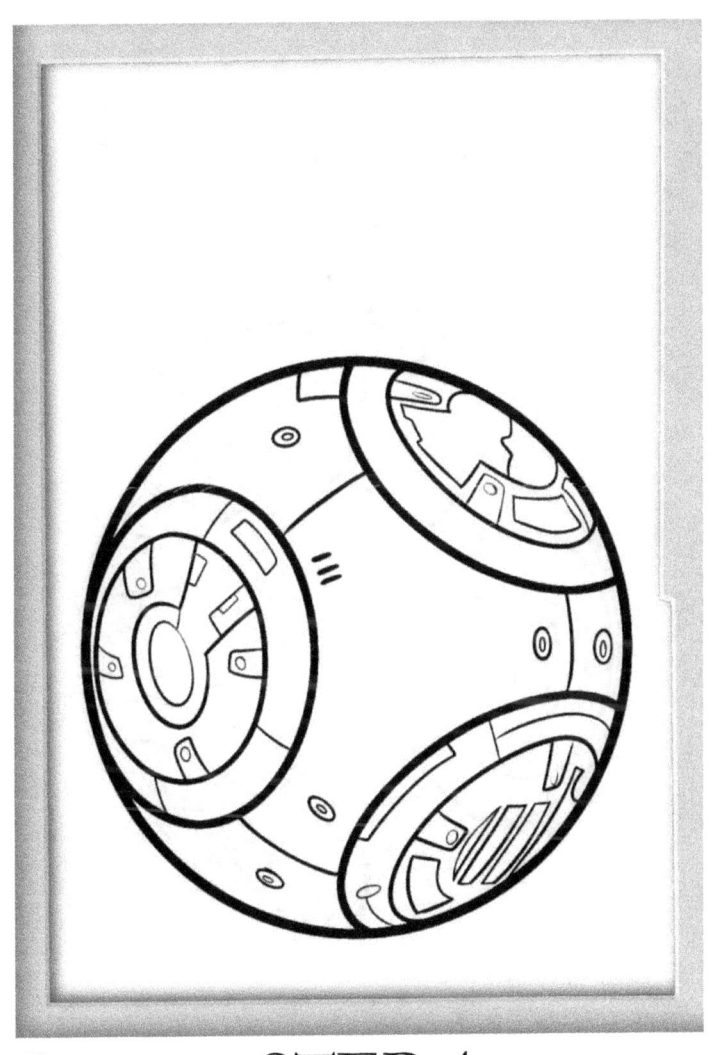

STEP 4

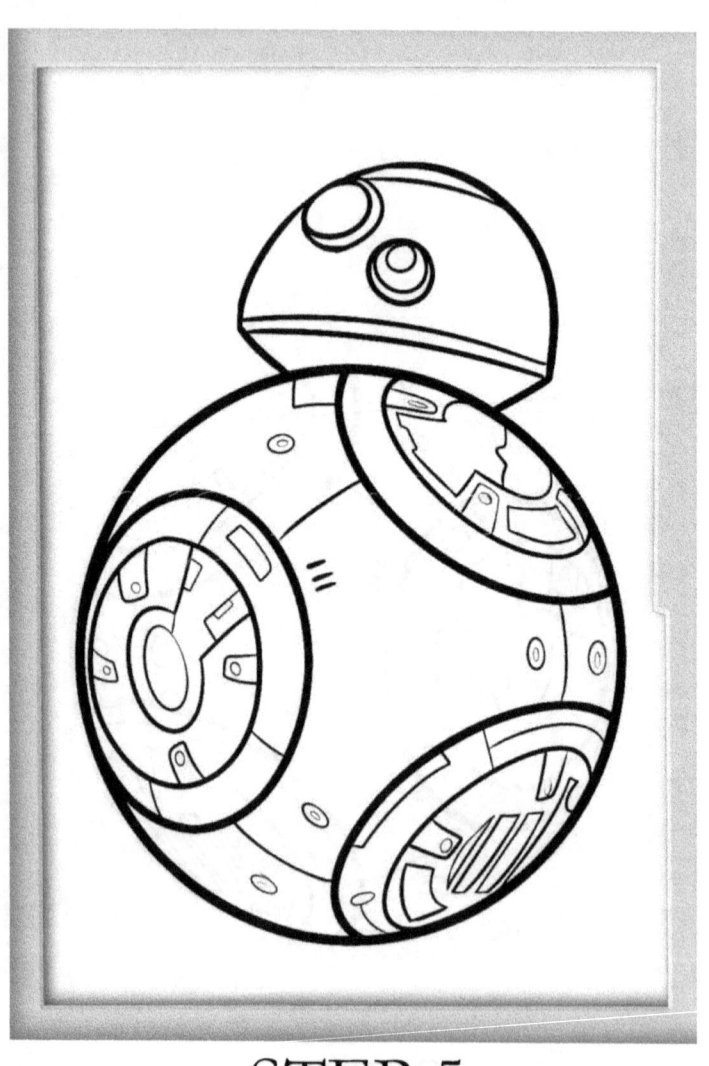

STEP 5

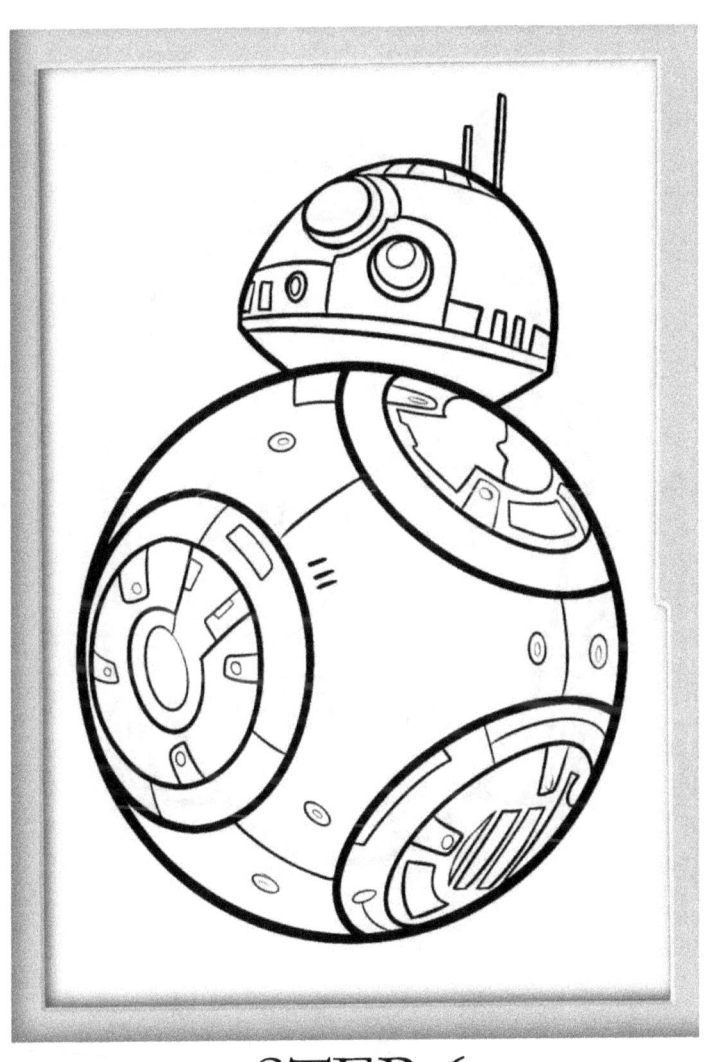

STEP 6

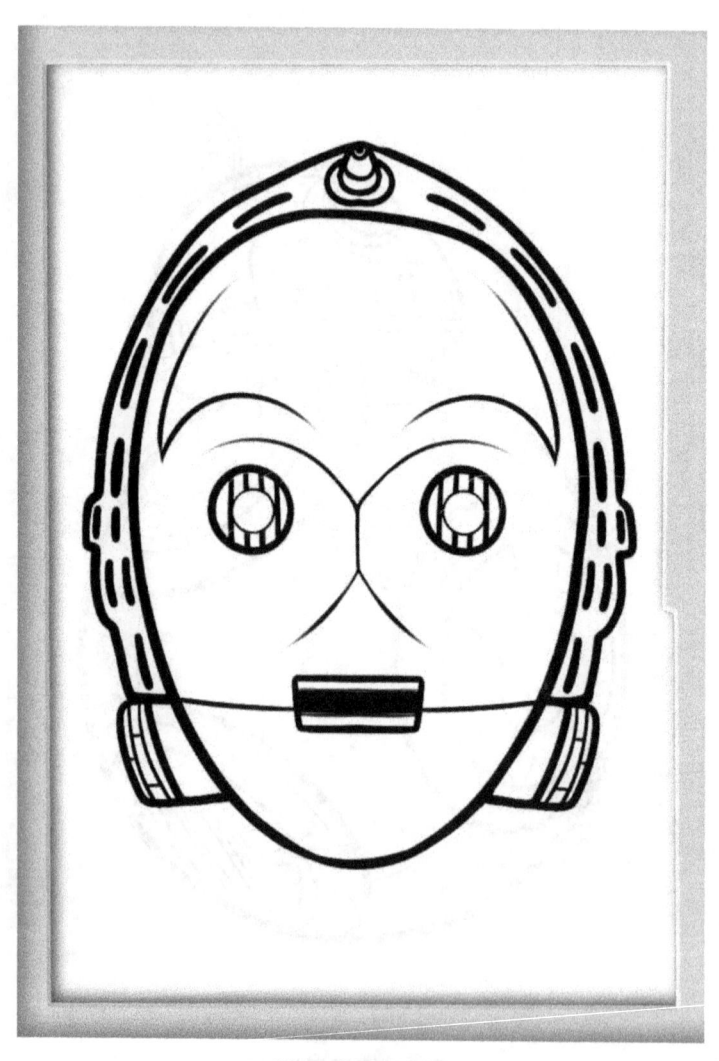

C-3PO

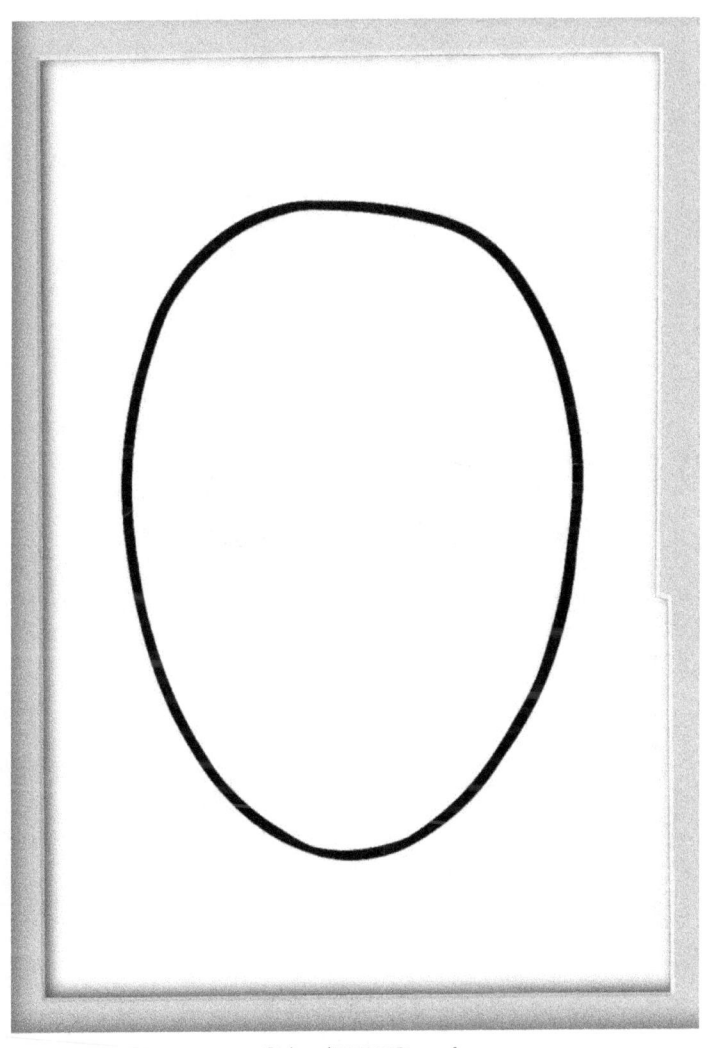

STEP 1

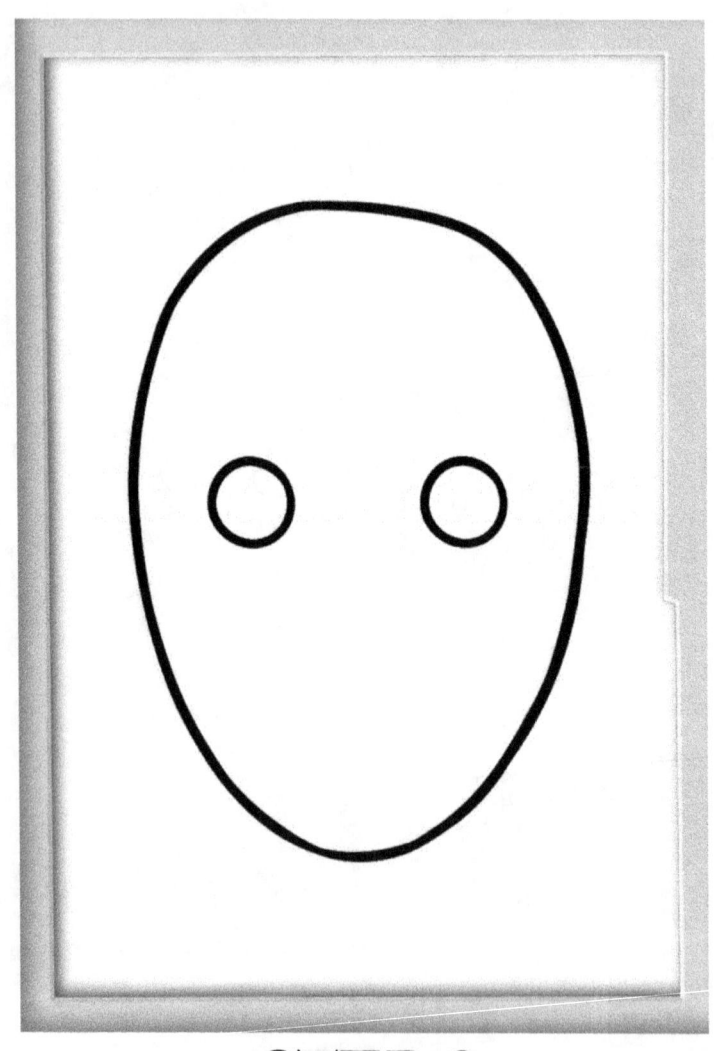

STEP 2

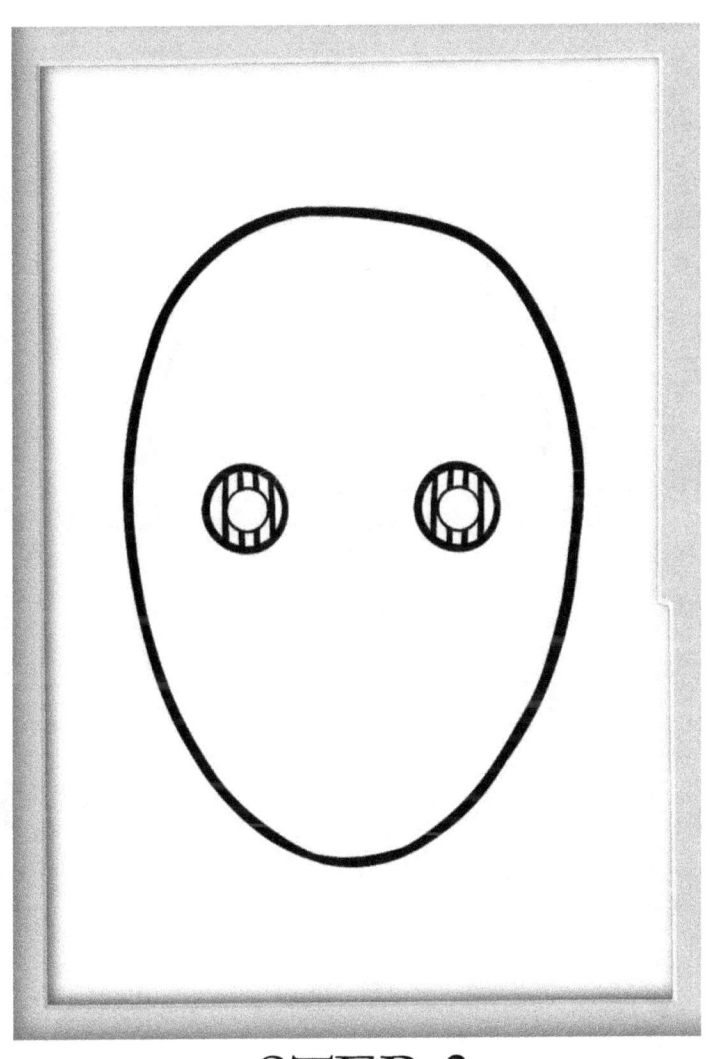

STEP 3

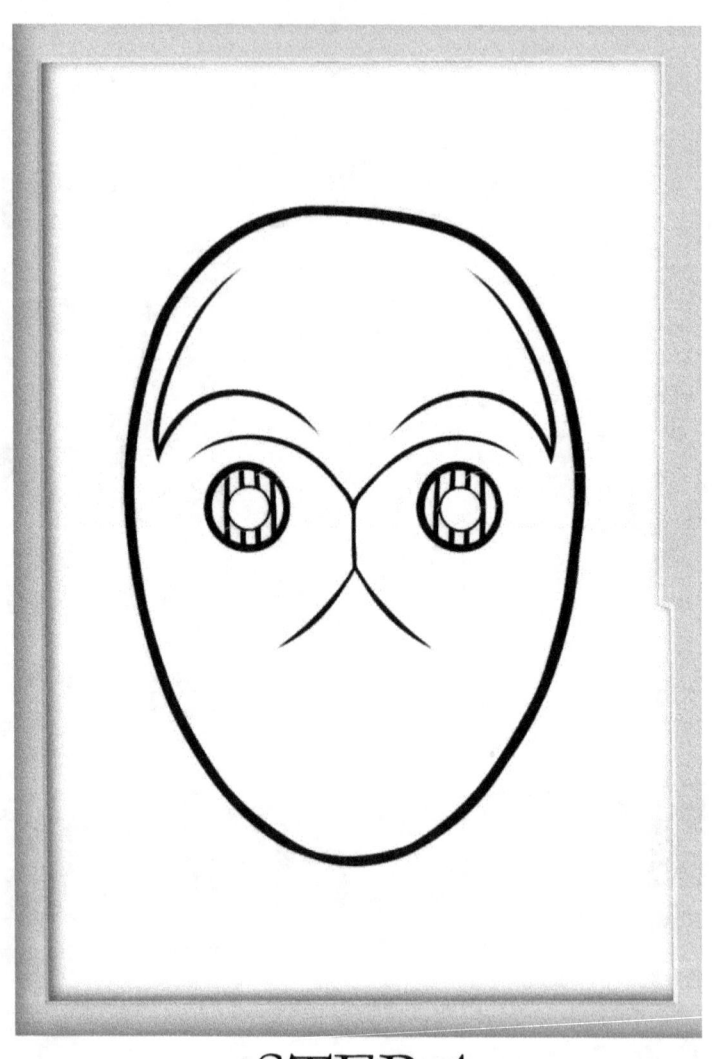

STEP 4

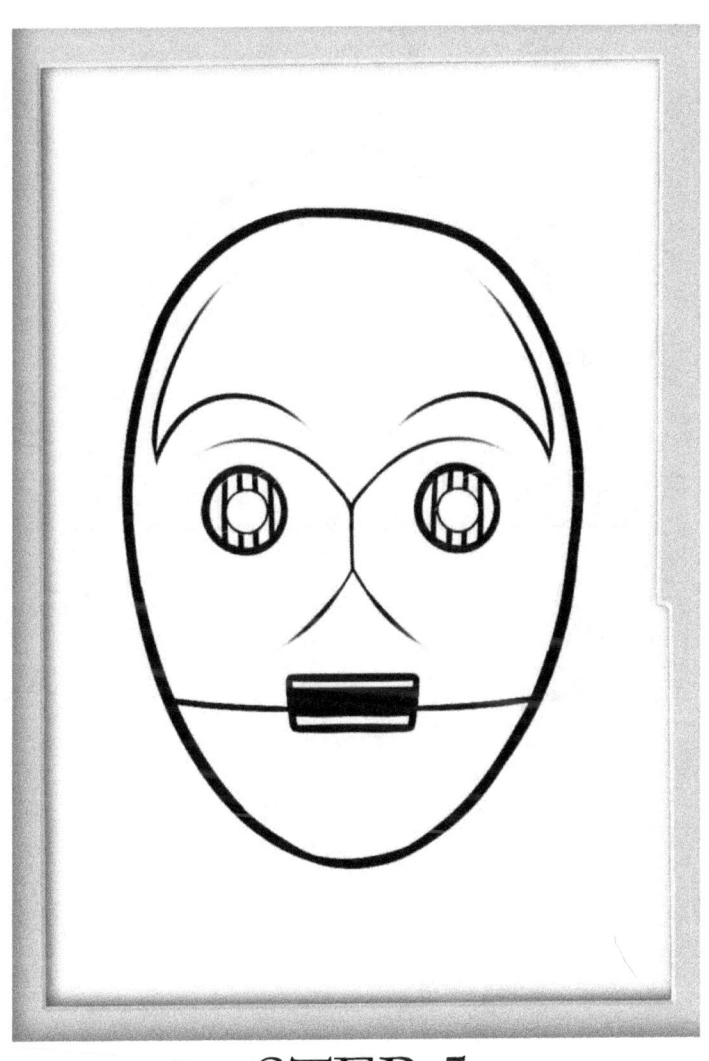

STEP 5

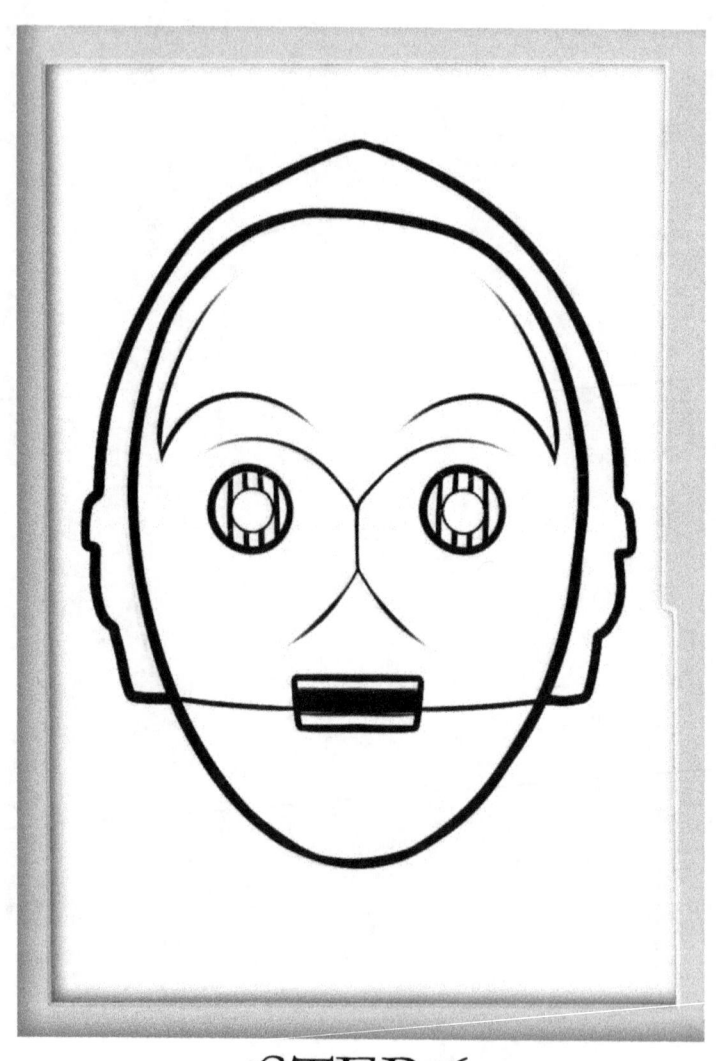

STEP 6

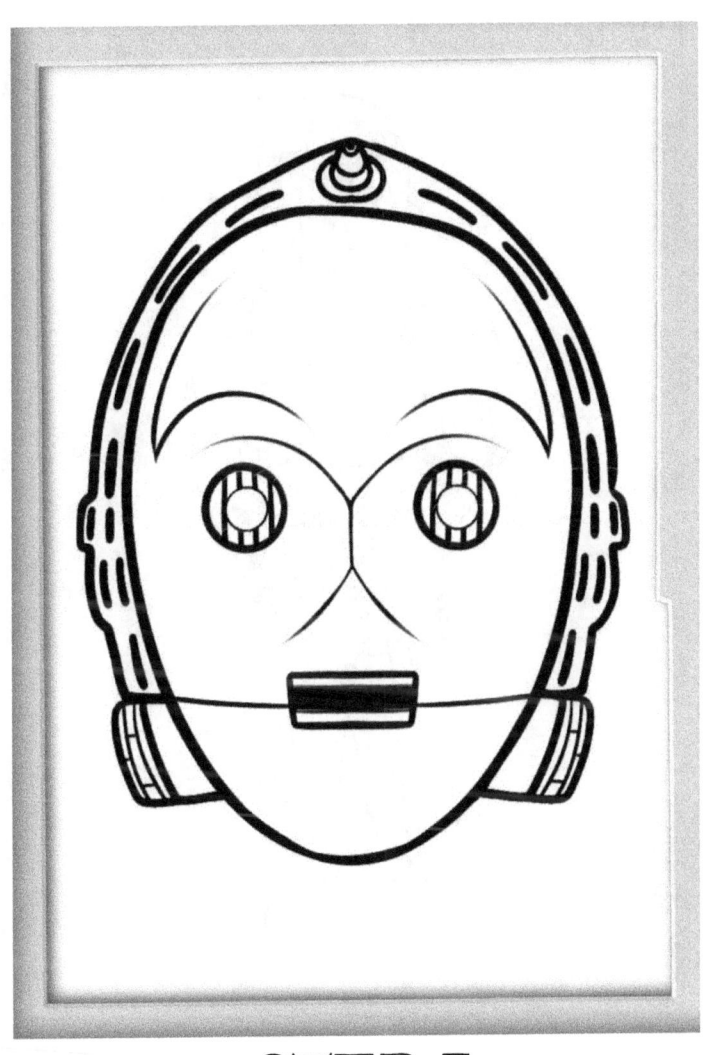

STEP 7

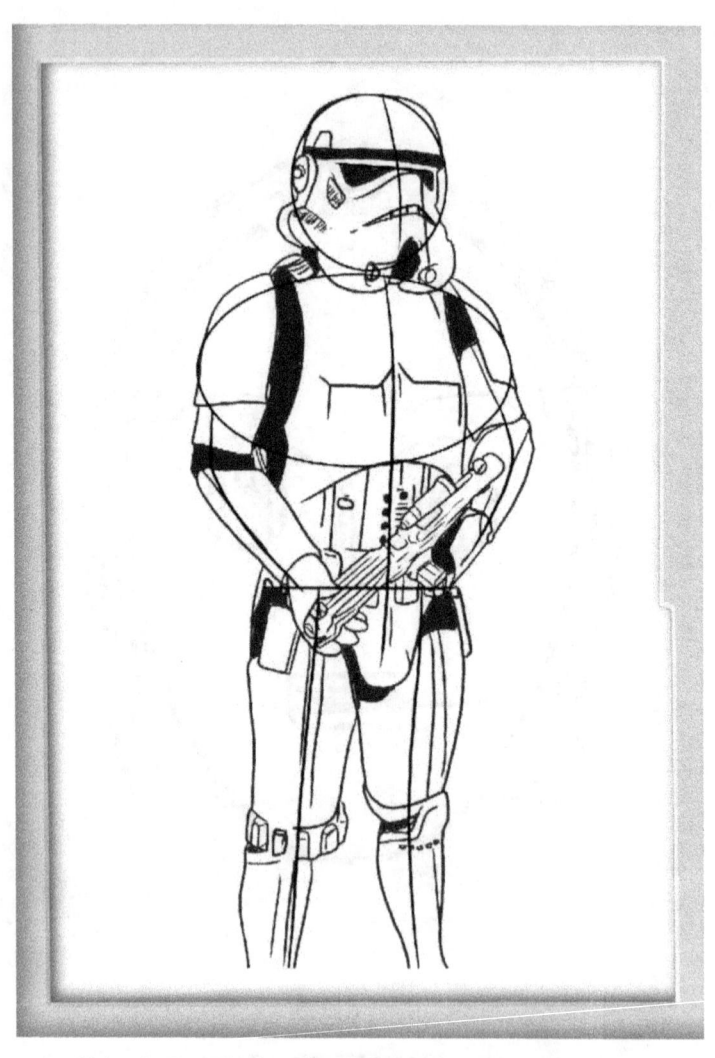

STORMTROOPER

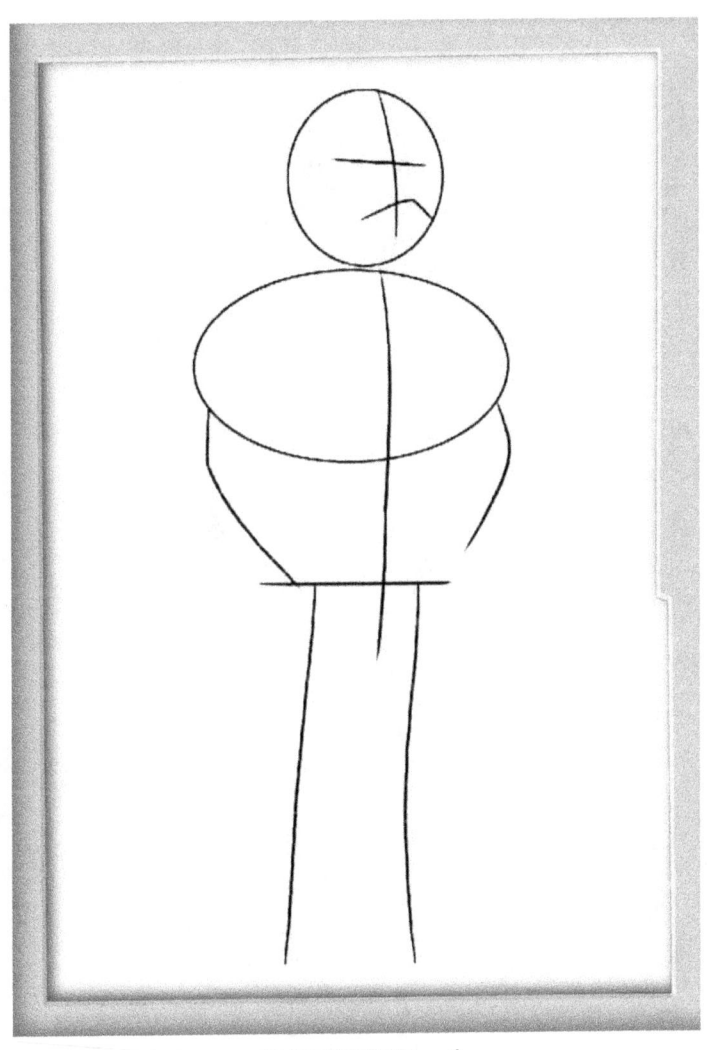

STEP 1

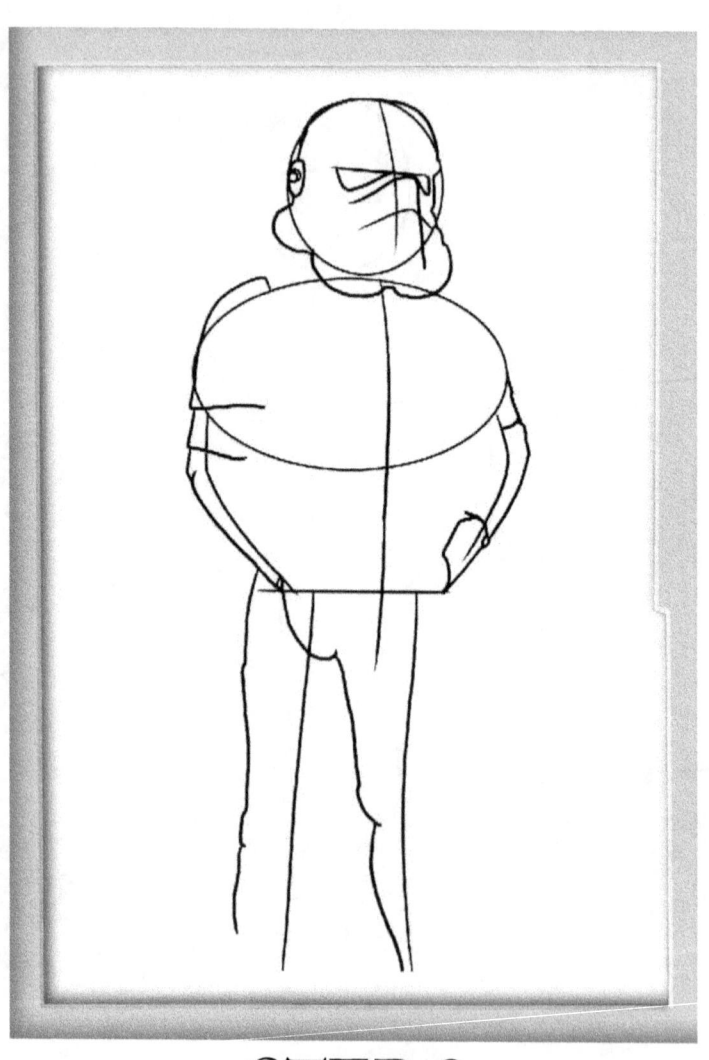

STEP 2

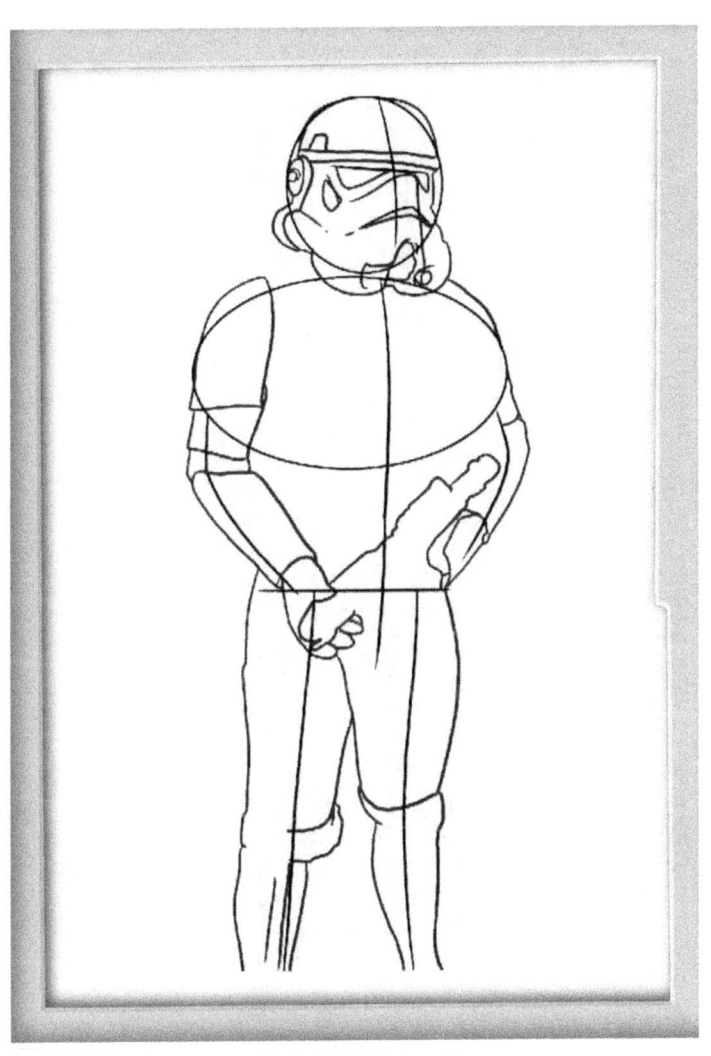

STEP 3

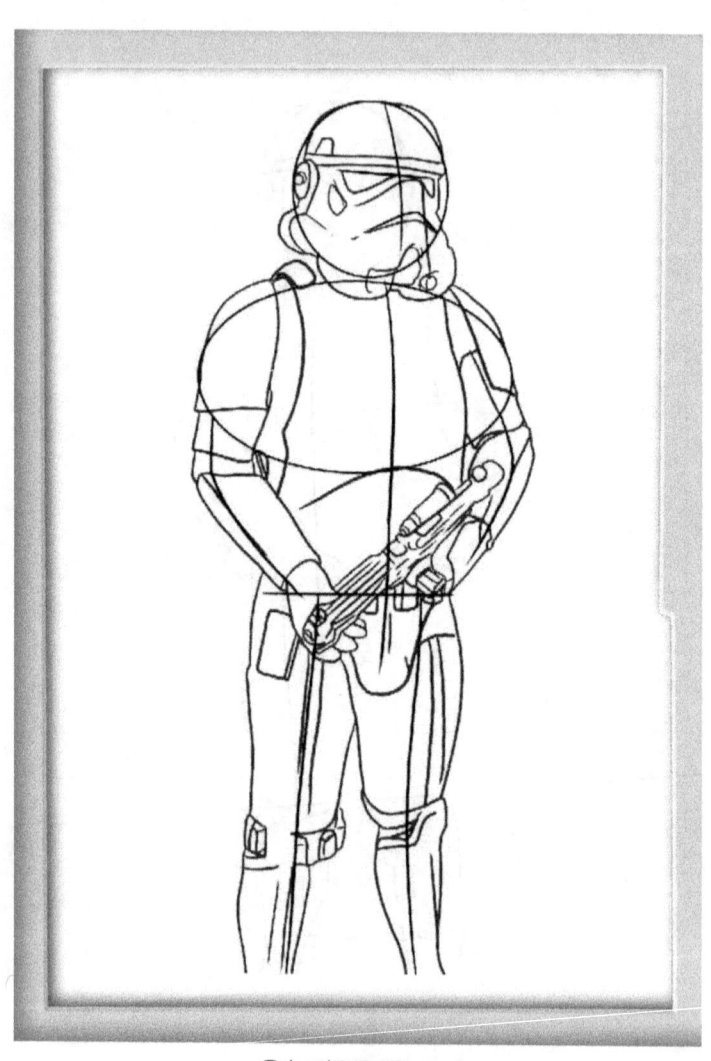

STEP 4

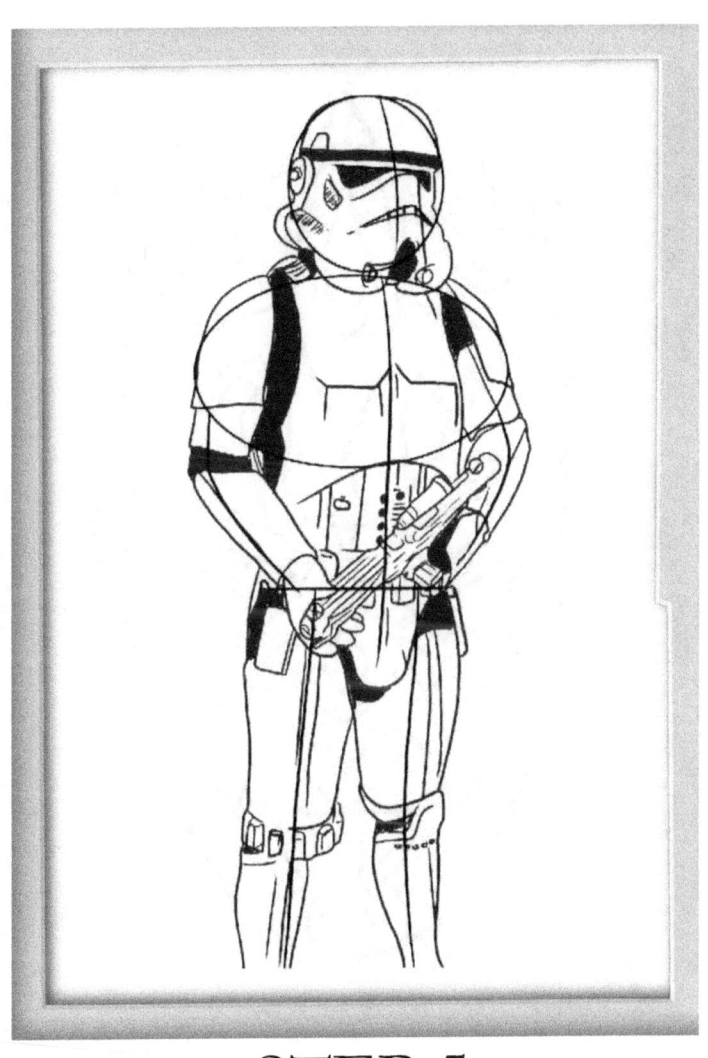

STEP 5

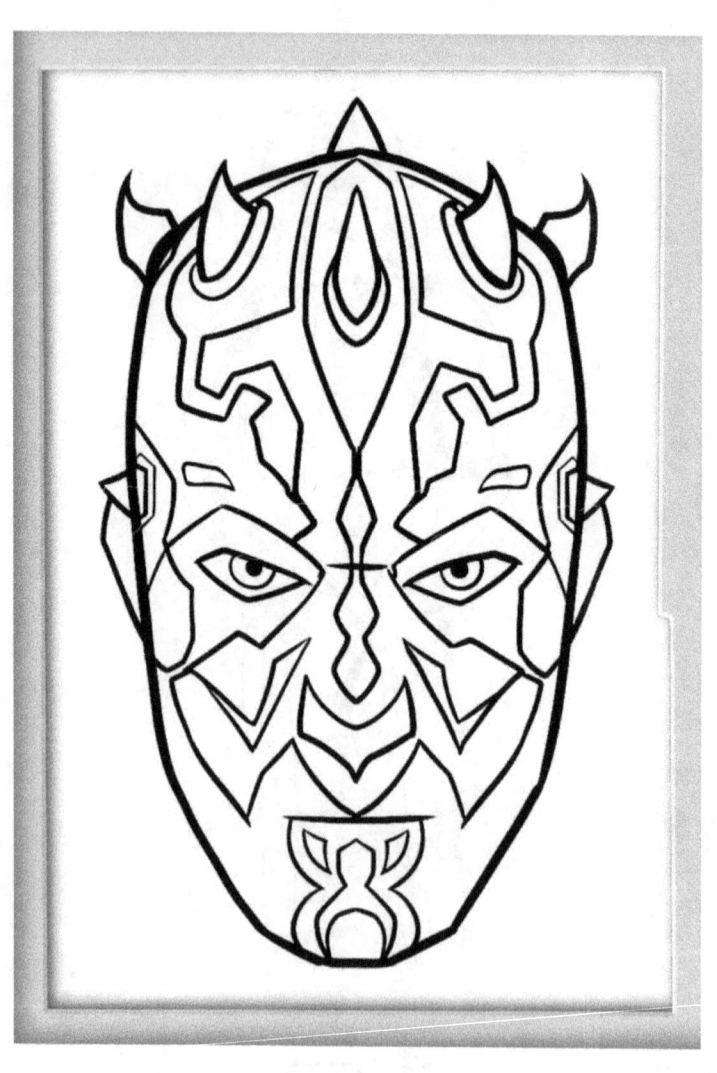

DARTH MAUL

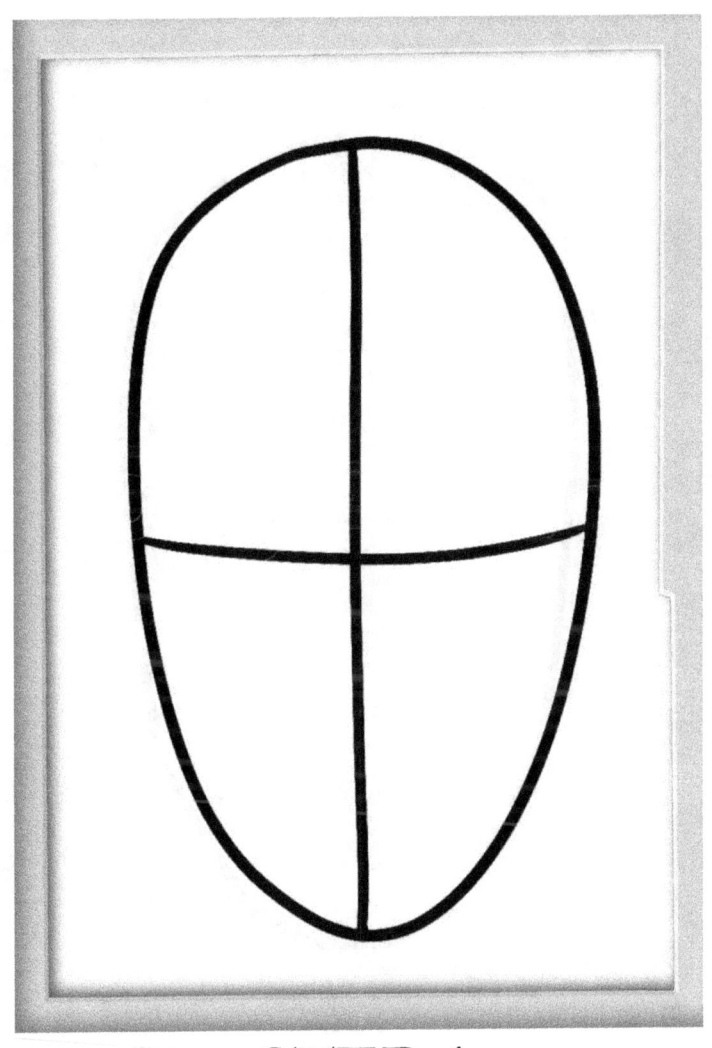

STEP 1

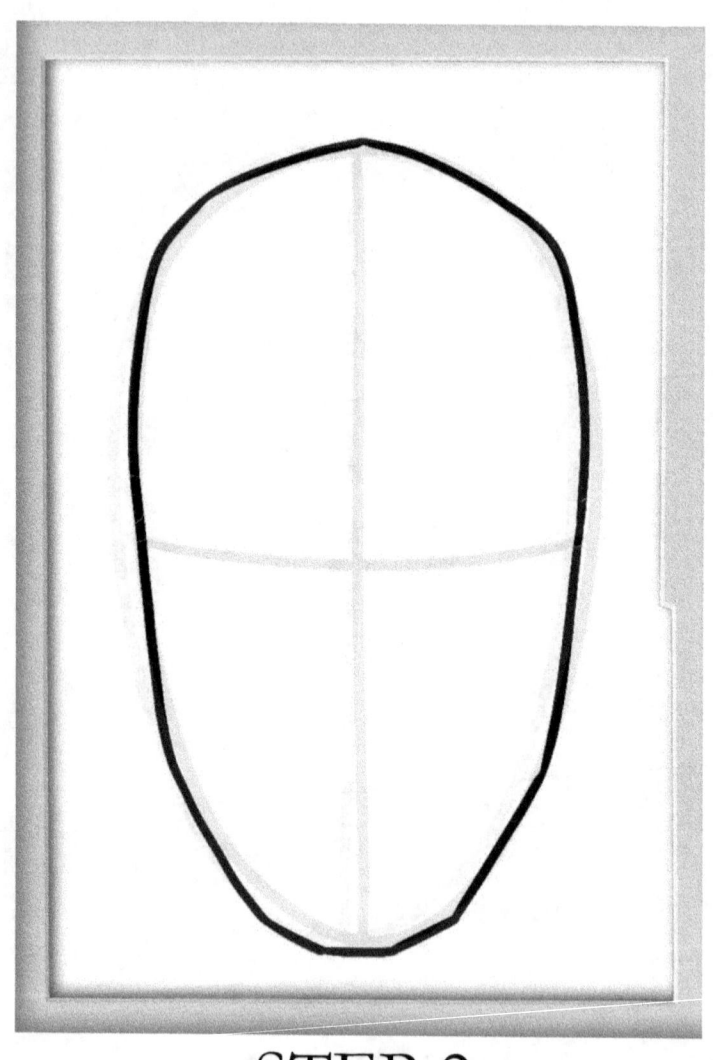

STEP 2

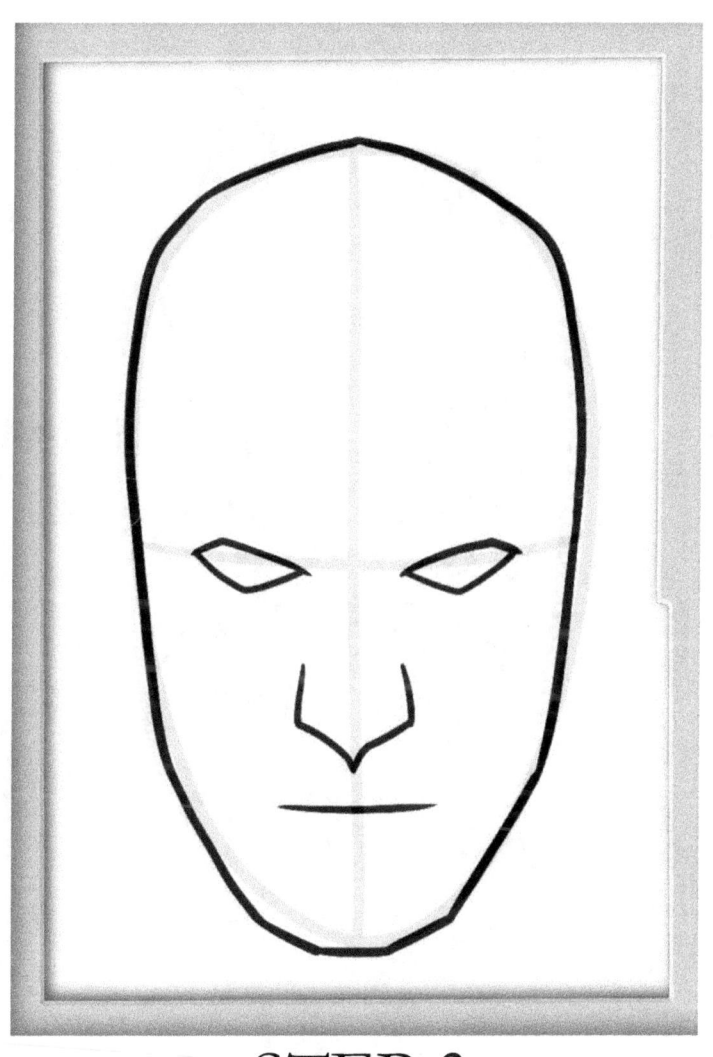

STEP 3

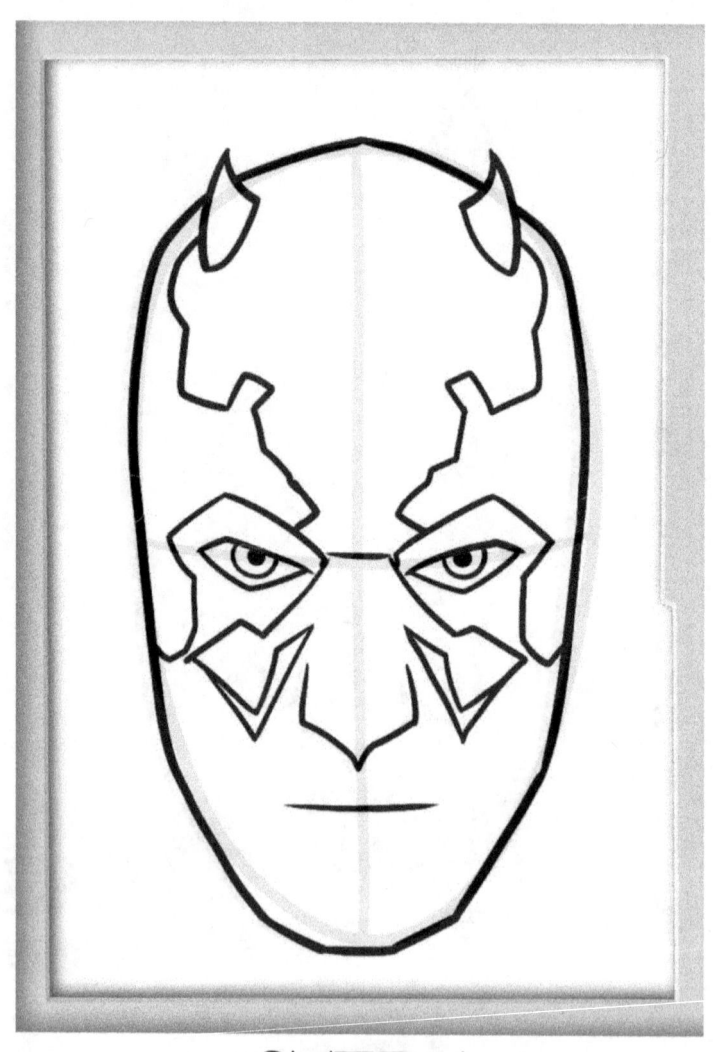

STEP 4

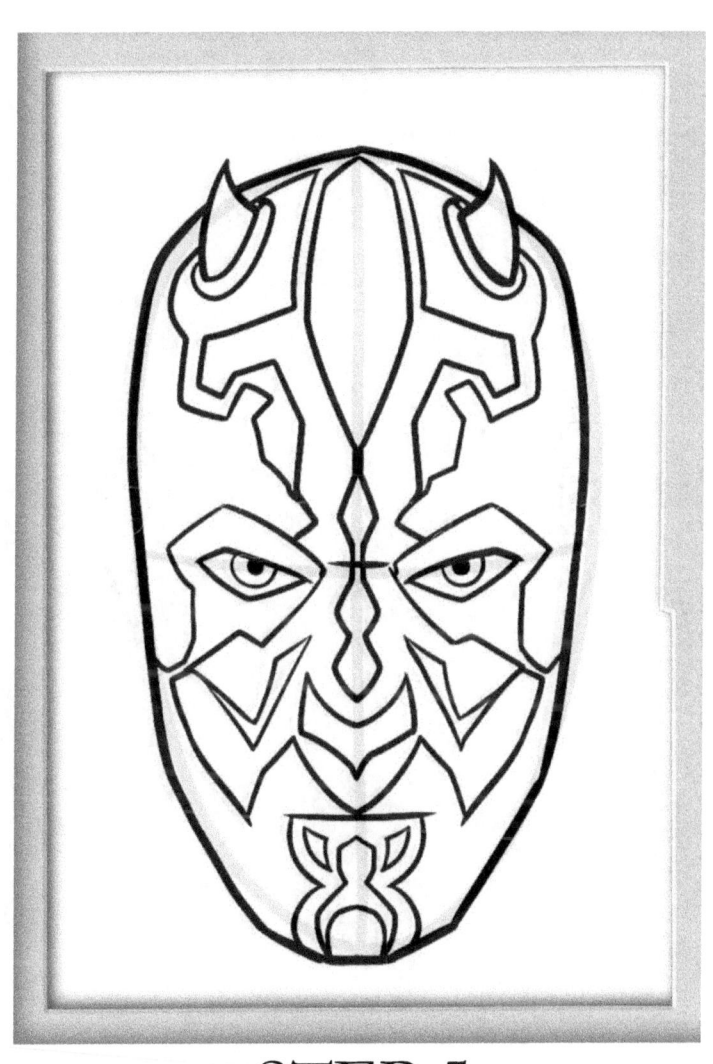

STEP 5

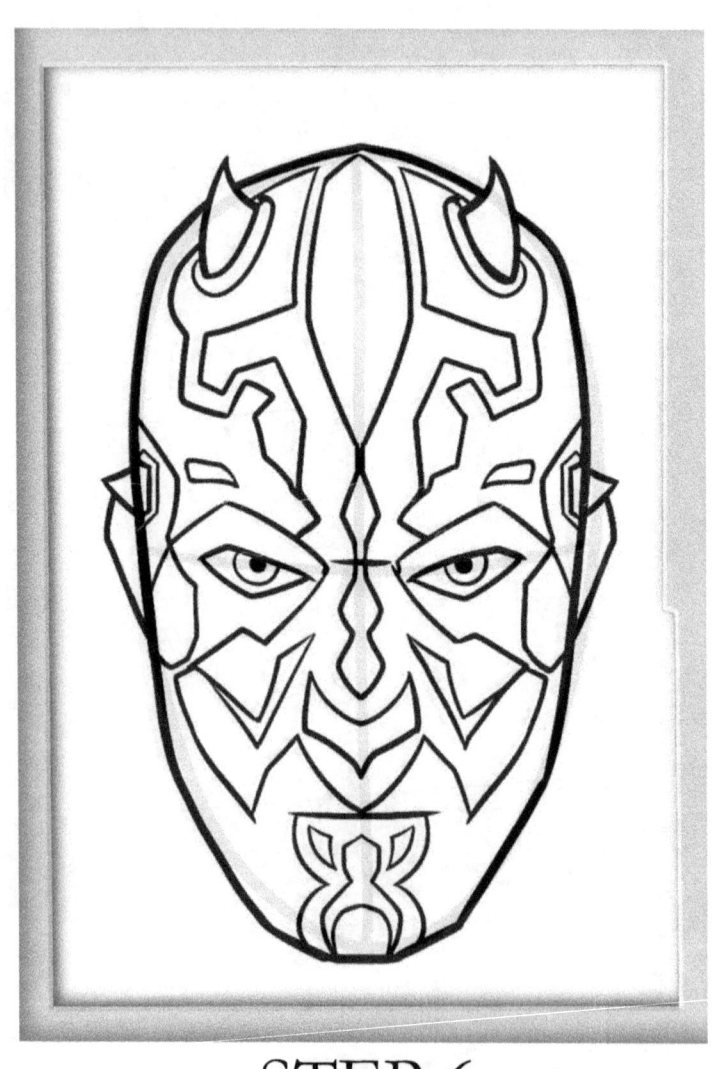

STEP 6

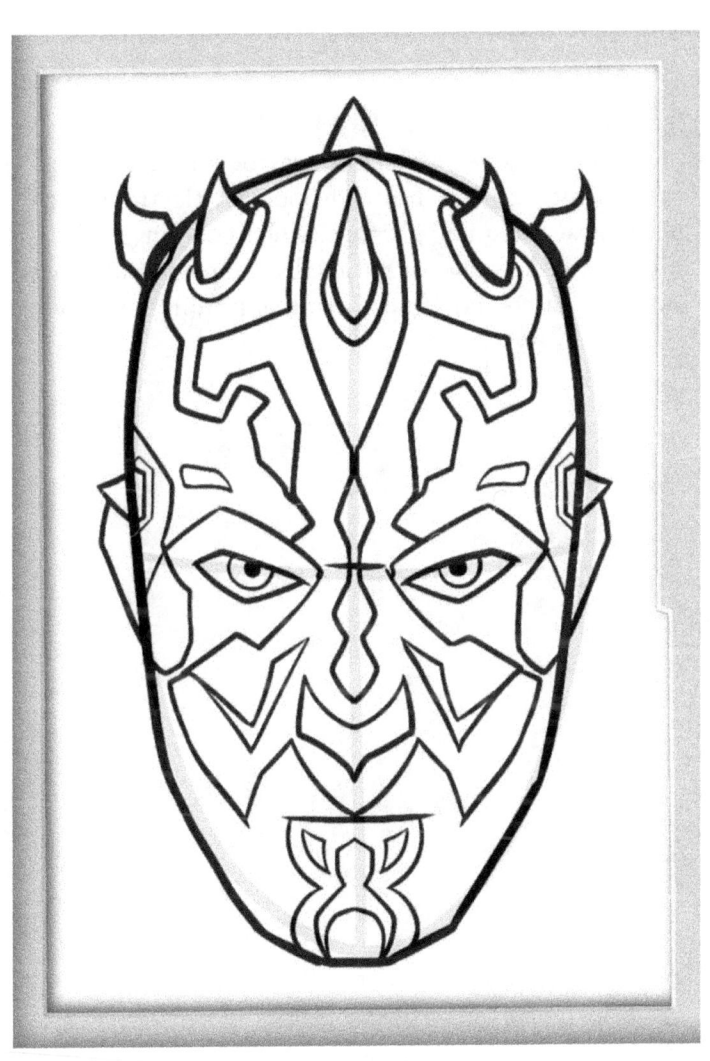

STEP 7

www.ingramcontent.com/pod-product-compliance
Lightning Source LLC
Chambersburg PA
CBHW071644170526
45166CB00003B/1432